# MOM's
# FIELD GUIDE

## What You Need to Know to Make It Through Your Loved One's Military Deployment

by Sandy Doell

WARRIOR ANGEL PRESS

©2006 Sandy Doell

Book and cover design by Marian Hartsough

ISBN-10: 1-932311-20-3
ISBN-13: 978-1-932311-20-4

Printed in the United States of America

10 9 8 7 6 5 4 3

WARRIOR ANGEL PRESS
1285 Stratford Avenue, Suite G262
Dixon, California 95620
866-221-8408
http://www.momsfieldguide.com

*To Peggy Buryj,*
*for whom fear became a reality*
*on May 5, 2004.*

**W**ith the *Mom's Field Guide,*" Sandy Doell has performed a tremendous service for the families and loved ones of our deployed service members. Her book picks up where family support groups leave off, providing an abundance of advice and guidance for those who are left behind, and often left wondering, "What can I do to help?" Most importantly, perhaps, is Sandy's message that a combat deployment is a team effort. As a soldier, airman or Marine, you simply can't fight effectively if you're worried about your family back home. As a spouse or a parent, getting through a deployment requires a special brand of courage and perseverance . . . the kind Sandy Doell certainly possesses. Getting through a deployment is never easy, but the *Mom's Field Guide* can be a great help along the way.

— Colonel John Fenzel, USA
May 28, 2007


Hi Sandy,

I just received your book, *Mom's Field Guide*, in the mail today! What a GREAT book. Thank you so much!!! I am a research person too and boy you sure could've saved me a lot of time if I would have gotten this book sooner! What a GREAT and VALUABLE resource book. My son is currently serving in Iraq. He has only been there for 2 months and their really is no way of explaining the emotional turmoil we ALL feel inside. Feelings of being so PROUD and such FEAR at the same time! What a Roller Coaster Ride we are on! I've only read half your book so far and I feel so comforted already to know that I am not alone. Thank you!

Sincerely,
Sunny
April 29, 2007

# Contents

# CONTENTS

# Part II
# Practical Matters 65

# CONTENTS

# CHAPTER 1

# Support Our Troops

## A Beautiful Day in August

The last strains of the "Star Spangled Banner" had not yet begun to fade when a cheer went up and clenched fists were raised all over the crowd of almost 62,000 people who had gathered to see the Belterra Casino 300, one of the races in the annual IRL circuit. No clouds interrupted the blue expanse of Kentucky sky that Sunday afternoon, August 15, 2004. I tried to wipe away the tears that had been trickling down my cheeks throughout the playing of the National Anthem, but as it ended, I couldn't help myself. I turned and sobbed against my husband Dave's chest.

Everyone around me was cheering for the good ol' U.S.A., feeling strong and expressing their patriotism, remembering 9/11. Support for our troops in Iraq and Afghanistan and around the world was almost palpable in that stadium. I knew that, and for the most part, I shared their sentiment. But I was feeling something most of the other fans weren't feeling that day—overwhelming fear for my son David, who spent 2004 in Babil Province in Iraq with the 66th MP Company, working to train and prepare the new Iraqi Police to provide security for their country. He had just e-mailed me that morning to say that his platoon was leaving Baghdad after some vehicle repairs and heading back to their base near Babylon.

1

The news for the past few days had been filled with the growing standoff in Najaf, centered on the Imam Ali Mosque there and especially in its nearby cemetery. I was afraid he was about to be sent to Najaf to join in that fight. I was afraid of the danger to him on the road between Baghdad and his home base. I was afraid of mortar attacks once he returned to the base. So, while I felt the same pride those race fans around me felt, in fact, more because my son was actually participating in the War on Terrorism, my pride was tempered with a good old-fashioned dose of fear for my child—something I know all mothers understand.

The irony wasn't lost on me that day. I cried for the same reason everyone else cheered. I'm sure there were others in that crowd who had family members in dangerous places, but I sure felt alone that day. The few who noticed me sobbing away against Dave's chest had no idea what prompted me to cry like that, and of course, they all looked the other way at such an embarrassing display of emotion. I probably would have done the same if I had witnessed such an outburst from a stranger in a crowded place.

I think that was the only time I broke down and cried all year, and I learned a very simple lesson that day: to avoid all patriotic music unless I was in a place where I didn't mind sobbing out loud. I could not listen to the National Anthem or especially to that Lee Greenwood song, "Proud to Be an American," without shedding a few tears. It all takes on a new meaning.

## The New Patriotism

Yard signs, bumper stickers, ribbon magnets on cars, yellow ribbons on trees, blue star banners on front doors, and flags flying in every other front yard—these symbols of our patriotism and belief in our country are on display everywhere. We haven't experienced such an overt outpouring of patriotism since World War II. We're all singing along about being "proud to be an American, where at least I know I'm free." We wear our pride on our chests in the form of T-shirts with patriotic slogans and on the bumpers of our cars. It's really touching the way we've all rallied 'round our men and women in uniform.

Freedom isn't free, however; neither can it be had for the price of a song, a T-shirt, or a bumper sticker—or even an e-mail. It's being paid for in flesh and blood and tears and plain old sweat at temperatures over 120 degrees.

It's also being paid for in another currency: the peace of mind of hundreds of thousands of people who live in your cities and neighborhoods, down the street and right next door. The families and loved ones of the soldiers serving in Iraq and Afghanistan don't wear desert camo, don't carry weapons, and don't need body armor—there's no armor that can protect our hearts from the pain of constant paralyzing fear.

The parents and families of people serving in Iraq appreciate all the flag waving. We appreciate that our spouses, sons and daughters, brothers and sisters, nephews, nieces, and grandchildren are not being treated in the shameful way this country treated its returning veterans from Viet Nam.

I was angry that sunny day in August, angry at all those patriotic people who could still go to a sporting event, stand for the flag, wave their beers in salute, and yet, seemed completely unaware of the very real danger that thousands of American service members were facing that very day. They cared, but not enough to pay more than superficial attention to the standoff that was threatening the lives of those soldiers and marines that day. I was mad at people who had those little ribbons on the backs of their cars, who wore T-shirts and waved flags. I was glad it wasn't like Vietnam when people threw things at returning soldiers and called them baby killers, but I was also thinking that most people had the form of patriotism down, but not the function. They were

3

waving flags, but flag waving doesn't actually win a war. Sacrifice wins wars, and I didn't think most people were quite so willing to do that, while some of us were forced into it. It's a voluntary military we have now, but the families don't volunteer; we're just as affected and just as trapped by circumstance as the families of the WWI and WWII and VN era soldiers, sailors, and marines who marched off to war because they were drafted. We didn't volunteer for this duty.

Perhaps it's because of the volunteer status of our current military, but even though this country is literally at war, that war has no more effect on the daily lives of most U.S. citizens than a sporting event, an NFL game or an IRL race. It's something we notice, something we express an opinion about, something we cheer about; and then we just get back to our barbecue, back to the kids, back to daily life and all that affects us in so much more direct a way than the war.

# They Also Serve

When I got home the day after that race, full of angst and worry over the situation in Najaf and worrying about what part my son was playing in it, my second priority was to get in touch with some people I knew who could understand, people who were walking that path with me, other parents and loved ones of the soldiers in David's company. (My first priority was to hear from David himself, but I had no control over that. All I could do was wait for a phone call or an e-mail.)

I was also worried about another family member. My cousin's son was serving in the Marine Corps, had just been deployed to Iraq, and was quite likely in or near Najaf himself. One small bright spot in all our lives was that David and Mat, we later heard, actually ran into each other in the heat and turmoil of that August in Najaf and shared a meal together. Another cousin's son and his wife were in the northern part of Iraq at the same time, near Mosul, so my husband and I had four family members to wonder and worry and pray about throughout 2004.

I learned a lot in 2004, I gained a lot of strength, a lot of patience. Not much can rattle me these days because I have already been rattled to the core. I also gained some lifelong friends. I have never met any of them face to face (although I plan to), but we are family. We walked a road together that most people never have to walk; we supported each other along the way with phone calls and e-mails. I know we would all have suffered a lot more without the friendship and support of what we came to refer to as our "Battle Buddies."

# The New Military Family

The current War on Terrorism presents us with a unique situation in our country's history. In past military conflicts, when there was a draft and every young man had to serve, everyone had someone who was fighting; everyone at least knew someone who had been sent to war. We were, so to speak, all in the same boat.

Now our military is "all volunteer"; it's their job to fight wars and our society can be thankful there are people willing to do that, but most of us don't have to do more than feel gratitude for their efforts or maybe say a prayer when we hear of a soldier's death in a war zone. What most of us feel is a generalized appreciation, not fear for a loved one.

Our servicemen and women come from all over the country, although I believe a preponderance of them come from the South, the Midwest, the Plains states, and the Southwest. They come from working class backgrounds, from farms and small towns, from depressed areas where jobs are scarce and the best way to find one is to leave home. If you're rich enough or smart enough or have good connections, you don't tend to volunteer for the military. There is also a certain type of person, what I call "the warrior type," who tends to enjoy the military life. David is one of those. He's the type who spent his youth sneaking off to go cliff diving or whitewater rafting or bungee jumping. In his words, "If something scares me, I want to do it." I'm really not sure I follow that logic, but I recognize it.

When he announced right after September 11, 2001, that he was joining the Army, I didn't like it, but I understood that it was important to him, and that the job of a soldier was his role in society. I had no idea then that I was going to be a "military mom," and have a few experiences of my own, none of which were pleasant. What they were was educational. I learned a lot that year, not intellectual stuff, but soul stuff. I learned to be patient, I learned to pray as I had never prayed before, and I learned to reach out to and become best friends with strangers who were having the same learning experience all across this country. I learned to analyze the situation I found myself in and try to make the best of it, to make myself a help and not a hindrance to my son, my cousins, and all their friends.

## Why I Wrote This Book

I realized about halfway through David's tour of duty in Iraq, that I was enlightened; I was one of the lucky ones because I knew how to do research, how to write letters, how to make educated guesses about whether he was involved in that day's news story. I found that, even though it seemed unfathomable that anyone could be any more frightened or upset by the whole situation than I was, that there were others who were in worse shape. I knew David was in Baghdad that day in August. I knew he was going back to Babylon. I knew that from there, he'd be in a good spot to be sent to fight in Najaf. I learned that others didn't have any idea of the distance between Najaf and Babylon. They might have had a loved one in Mosul and been afraid that he or she could be sent to Najaf—unlikely because of the distance.

I wrote this book, first and foremost, for those others who are even less able to handle their fear than I was because they don't have the research skills I have, don't know how to search for information, don't know how to find a detailed map of Iraq, and don't know how to search the Internet for up-to-date and accurate news stories.

In this book I share everything I learned about how to search for information, who you can approach for help in certain circumstances, how you can get in touch with other families and how you can support each other through tough times. You'll learn basic things about time zones, geography, differences in climate, news reporting methods, military procedures, and more that will help you know where your loved one is. You'll learn communication methods that will help you stay in contact. You'll learn when to be worried and when you can be relatively sure that all is well. You'll learn military jargon where a simple word like "busy" carries connotations you might not realize, where a "mission" is quite different from an "operation," and such terms as v-bid and d-fac and toc are tossed around so fast, you forget to ask what they mean.

Most importantly, you will learn how to do a few things that give your soldier the support he or she needs from home. The things you do for your loved one will also give you a sense of purpose that will help immensely when all you want to do is wring your hands and cry.

I wrote this book, secondly, for the rest of the country, for those who feel patriotic but don't know where to begin to express that patriotism—or maybe just lack sufficient inspiration to make more than a beer-waving gesture.

I wrote this book to tell those family members with loved ones in harm's way and those patriots who want to express their thanks to the military members and their families some specific things they can do, giving full instructions for each activity, that will actually give support to the troops and help those of you here at home, not just feel that you are doing something useful and constructive and supportive, but actually do it in a real way. (You can pray and worry, I guess, but "faith without works is dead," according to the Bible, and it's the "work" that helps to pass the time.) If the rest of the country, those without loved ones at war, get an idea or two and put something in motion, all the better.

The most important thing I learned during my son's year in a war zone: by reaching out to him and others in his company, and to those other family members and their buddies in Iraq, I was also doing something positive for myself. Work is an antidote to worry, and I believe that one home-baked cookie or one CD or book might just help to lift one soldier's spirits enough that for a critical moment he can pay attention, be alert instead of down in the dumps, and so in just that one small way, maybe I could help to save a life.

In chapters 2 and 3, you'll learn all about mail and CARE packages, how to send them, what to send, everything I learned over the course of a year about sending mail to military men and women deployed in the Middle East.

# PART I

# Covering the Basics

Your job for the duration of your soldier's deployment will be to provide all the love and contact with home that you can. You'll do this by sending letters, pictures, cards, and other reminders of home. Chapters 2 and 3 cover all that you'll need to know to keep a steady supply of mail coming to your soldier. Mail from home (letters, boxes, parcels, packages) is mentioned by nearly every deployed soldier as the one thing they look forward to most of all.

Taking care of this most important task is going to be one of your best coping mechanisms too. You may feel helpless as you watch your loved one get on the plane to go and do a difficult job under uncomfortable and dangerous conditions. But you also have a job to do in support of your child, relative, or friend who is in harm's way. You have to start immediately making sure he knows that he is loved and thought of daily at home. Your job is to keep him feeling connected.

E-mail, instant messaging, and phone calls will help maintain the contact with home and family that helps your soldier stay physically and mentally healthy, but even though hearing your voice is uplifting for them (and vice versa), a letter that they can take out and read again and again is the most welcome thing they'll receive.

Deployed soldiers also enjoy receiving mail from more distant relatives and friends, so be sure to share his address with everyone in the family and encourage everyone to write. Especially welcome are letters from children.

<u>**One word of caution**</u>: Do not share the addresses of military personnel on public Web sites or with anyone you do not know. In the past, writing to a soldier you didn't know was considered the patriotic thing to do. Now it's dangerous to share their addresses, so make sure you know the person you are giving the address to, and make sure you have the service member's permission to share his address. Use good judgment about this. There are crazy people doing bad things these days, and it's sad, but you have to be vigilant about the information you share with strangers.

In Chapter 2, "Supplies," you'll learn all about what to send. In Chapter 3, "To the Post Office," you'll learn how to send the things you've carefully chosen, and all about writing letters to deployed soldiers. There are a few considerations to keep in mind when you sit down to write and preparations to take before you pack that box that will make the mail experience easier for you and uplifting for your deployed family member.

# CHAPTER 2

# Supplies

FROM: David

DATE: Saturday, September 11, 2004, 1:40 p.m.

TO: Mom

SUBJECT: Cookies

As far as cookies go, I would like to get some Chips
Ahoy or some home-made peanut butter cookies with
Hershey Kisses on them. That would be great. I got
all of those packages that you have sent. I got one
with Twinkies and cupcakes, and I got the one with
Scott's CD in it and all of the pictures.

I went out today to the Babylon ruins and took about
52 pictures from the outside and the inside. Now I
have to install the program for my camera and then
I can send them to you. We are making plans with one
of the interpreters to take us to the tower of Babil
and I'll get some pictures of that too.

Okay, I have to go and get ready for tomorrow, but
I'm gonna try and call you first. Thanks for all of
the packages; the stuff I get really helps cope with
being in this place. If I didn't get them, I think
I would be depressed and have nothing to do.

Okay, I love you, I'll talk to you later, and c-ya soon.

# The Benefits of Regular Mail

Mail not only gives your deployed soldier some of the daily supplies and comfort items he needs, it also helps keep him entertained, gives him a taste of home, and helps to stave off loneliness, boredom, and depression. Most important of all, it reminds him that he is loved and cared for by people back home. In fact, deployed military men and women can survive quite well without home-baked goodies, pictures, and news from home. But, oh, what a difference it makes to their morale to get it!

You want to keep a steady supply of mail and packages arriving. My goal was for David to never miss a mail call without receiving a package of some kind. He got mail from other people in the family and from friends as well, but my own personal goal was to send a package once a week. Sometimes it was a challenge to think of novel and interesting things to send. Occasionally, I succeeded in finding unique and fun stuff. Other times, my packages weren't quite so "inspired," but I sent one once a week anyway.

The Internet is awash in lists of suggested items to send to deployed soldiers. Most of those lists date from early in the Iraq deployment. Some of the items they include, such as toilet paper and sample sizes of toiletries, are outdated now that the troops have more permanent dwelling places and better access to PXs where they can buy the things they need for themselves. You will have to use your own judgment when choosing what to send to your loved one, but for the most part, things have changed since 2003 when those lists were first posted. I will provide some lists of suggested items to send in this chapter, but you will want to tailor these lists to fit the needs of your soldier and his current living arrangements. You'll also add to and subtract from your list as you receive requests or learn what meets with a positive response.

Just keep in mind that you need to be flexible in your planning, and ask your soldier what he needs and wants. He may not think to even ask for a needed item unless you remind him that you are packing boxes on a regular basis and really want to send him only things he wants and needs or will enjoy.

## Food to Send

We've all heard about the horrors of military food, of MREs (meals-ready-to-eat) and of de-fac (dining facility; aka mess) cooking. Since the infamous C-rations of World War II, Korea, and Viet Nam, the food has improved immensely. Still, it can be boring, and your deployed military family member is going to appreciate more than anything the food items you send to bolster his diet as well as his morale.

In fact, I believe the military does serve the troops a healthy, well-balanced diet. Often, however, a soldier goes to the same de-fac day after day, sees the same menu served day after day, and opts for the same choice every day because there are only one or two items that he likes. Even though they're being offered a variety of food, individual taste dictates that they aren't necessarily eating a balanced diet. You can help by sending food items you know they like. Send vitamins too, just to be on the safe side.

Find out whether your soldier has a microwave, a refrigerator, or a toaster available nearby. If he does, you can tailor your shipments to include things like microwave popcorn or freezer pops. One mother sent a microwave baking dish and then sent regular shipments of cake mixes designed for the microwave; the soldiers in her son's squad enjoyed brownies and cakes baked in the microwave.

The following food items are excellent choices if your soldier happens to be in a place where the food is not so good or his choices are limited. These can help to liven up an otherwise bland menu:

- **Tuna** It's best to get the kind that comes in an envelope. It doesn't need to be drained, and in a pinch can be eaten right out of the package. It also weighs less than the canned kind, so it's less expensive to send in your CARE packages. When you send tuna, be sure to send some individual packages of mayonnaise or salad dressing, pickle relish, a bowl to mix it in, and a fork and knife for mixing and spreading the resulting tuna salad on crackers. (Of course, send the crackers with the tuna too.)

  There's also chicken and turkey that come in envelopes at the grocery store. Chicken salad and tuna salad kits complete with crackers, mayo, and relish are also good and convenient.

- **Beef jerky** Be sure to check the labels of beef jerky. Some "beef" jerky actually contains pork, which you aren't allowed to send to Muslim countries.

- **Crackers** Send these along with tuna and peanut butter, jelly, or jars of cheese spread.

- **Peanut butter** Everybody enjoys peanut butter. It is included in the MREs, but nothing beats the brand names you know your soldier likes best. I just knew David would rather have Jif than whatever it was the Army was giving him.

- **Individual packets of jelly and mayo, salsa, relish,** whatever you can find that will help to liven up the dining facility fare, which can range in quality from mediocre to outstanding in various locations. Even though most military personnel in Iraq and Afghanistan now have access to freshly prepared food, they still go out on patrol and occasionally still find themselves having an MRE meal. These little packets can liven up the bland taste of the MREs.

■ **Cereal**  This, of course, is available in the de-fac and in the MREs, but you know your soldier's favorite brand, and that may not be available to him every day. Again, ask what he prefers if necessary. I knew David liked Golden Grahams and Fruity Pebbles, and every time I found individual size boxes of those, a few went into his CARE package that week.

■ **Instant oatmeal**  This was one of David's favorites. It was easy for him to just carry his packet of maple-flavored instant oatmeal to the de-fac, mix it up with some hot water, and have one of his favorite breakfasts.

■ **Cookies**  You know what his favorites are. In the e-mail that begins this chapter, David particularly mentions Chips Ahoy and homemade Peanut Butter Kisses. Chips Ahoy were a good choice because they didn't suffer so much from the heat. The homemade peanut butter cookies with Hershey Kisses would never have survived the heat in September though. During the cooler winter months, you can send more chocolate, but most of the year the desert heat makes its survival somewhat iffy.

You can buy tins at thrift stores for about $1 each to ship homemade cookies in. Line the tin with a large Ziploc bag, pack in the cookies, compress out as much air as possible, and seal the bag. Pad the tin with wadded up paper towels to keep the cookies from bouncing around. Put the lid on the tin, tape it down to secure, and most cookies will stay fresh and edible.

- **Candy**  Send hard candy, chewy candy, gum. Most of the year, you'll have to avoid chocolate because of the heat (can't say that too often). M&Ms are usually safe though. Luckily, it's all right to send chocolate during the Christmas season because the temperature drops considerably in the winter months.

- **Breakfast bars**  These are good. They're a convenient source of healthy grains, and most of them taste pretty good. They're healthier than a candy bar, filling, and tasty.

- **Protein and energy bars**  Some of these are better tasting than others, but all are a good source of needed vitamins, minerals, and energy.

- **Rice Krispie squares**  the pre-packaged kind always shipped well. Sometimes David requested the homemade kind, and we tried it a few times, but I recommend sticking to the ones you can pick up in the store already boxed up and prepared. They are almost as good as homemade, and they stay fresh longer.

- **PopTarts**  Stick with the foods you know they love. Depending on his living arrangements, your soldier might even have a toaster available, but if he doesn't these handy little items stay fresh for a long time and taste good even untoasted.

- **Cheese crackers**  A quick and easy snack.

- **Salsa**  A favorite item. You can buy it in microwaveable tubs. There are also varieties with cheese. Don't forget to include the chips for dipping and a spoon for stirring.

- **Cup cakes**  Homemade cakes don't survive the usual two-week trip to the Middle East, but Hostess Twinkies, Ding Dongs, chocolate cup cakes, and Dolly Madison

Zingers were favorites and have preservatives that make them good candidates for long trips. All the Little Debbie varieties also ship well. Once during the hottest part of the year, the filling in some Twinkies turned to an unappetizing yellow liquid, but most of the time this was a highly shippable item.

■ **Spreadable cheese** (Cheez Whiz or Old English). "Real" cheese was one of only a few requests for particular items that I got from my son. Dairy products are not abundant to troops deployed in the Middle East, and they develop a yearning for cheese, milk, ice cream, and yogurt.

Homemade goodies are much appreciated, but make sure what you bake and send will survive two weeks of heat and still be edible—cookies and trail mix are good. I've included some tested and tried recipes later in this chapter.

You might want to consider going to a restaurant supply house or wholesale grocer to buy boxes of individual packets of jelly, mayo, pickle relish, or other condiments. It can be hard to find enough of these that are free for the taking without feeling that you're overstepping the bounds of a restaurant or deli owner's hospitality. I have to say though that whenever I told deli clerks or grocery store cashiers what I wanted it for, they were unfailingly generous.

Still, you might find it easier to just buy a whole box and keep it handy to ship as needed. I bought a box of those little restaurant packets of grape jelly because I sent that almost every week until David moved to a camp where it was available. I sent mayonnaise often too, but I found that when I bought the packets of tuna in the grocery store, the store's deli would give me mayo to go with it. Again, people are very generous when you tell them why you need condiments.

If there's a microwave near your soldier's quarters, you can buy warm-up-able containers of beef stew, beefaroni, all sorts of items that he might prefer over the de-fac food and that are quite likely to be better than MREs. Browse around in the canned meat aisle of the grocery store. Mostly, check with your soldier. Chances are the food he's being served is quite edible and tasty. If it is, you can send more snack and fun food items and fewer of the staples.

Fun foods might include:

- **Candy, gum, mints, licorice, Life Savers**

- **Individually wrapped fruit snacks**

- **Sunflower seeds, nuts**

- **Kool-Aid**, the kind with sugar. They need the calories, and they need something to help spark up the quantities of water they must drink each day to keep their bodies hydrated.

- **Gatorade powder mix.** This is a good choice because it provides extra nutrients and is especially good for hydration.

- **Instant coffee and tea.** Starbucks has a plan that allows each employee to donate a pound of coffee a week to deployed military personnel. You might want to ask at your local coffee shop. People really would like to help; they just need to be pointed toward a needy soldier sometimes.

- **Bread sticks.** The kind you find on the top shelf in the salad dressing section, up there with the croutons and bacon bits. They're a crunchy alternative to pretzels and chips.

- **Individual servings of ranch dressing** to go with the bread sticks. This too is available in the salad dressing aisle, and the small container is just enough for one person to snack on. No need to refrigerate an unopened bottle of salad dressing after the snack.

- **Pringle's-type canned potato chips.** These don't crush the way regular ones do, and they're available now in practically every flavor.

- **Small containers of the kind of chip dip** that doesn't need to be refrigerated.

## Cookies

Just about any cookie recipe you have that isn't too gooey, chewy, or chocolate-y will ship well. One favorite standby was any variation of Oatmeal or Oatmeal Raisin Cookies. Anything based on an oatmeal cookie recipe with coconut, butterscotch chips, white chocolate chips, just about any drop or pressed cookie will ship well. Bar cookies and brownies probably won't stay fresh.

### CAUTION

Use only clear plastic wrap. Don't use the new colored stuff. In extreme heat, the colored plastic wrap imparts a smell to the food you wrap with it.

Home baked cookies are very much appreciated, but if you don't have time for baking in addition to shopping for all the other contents of a CARE package, boxing it up, and getting it to the post office, then by all means, send store bought snacks. Better to send a box every week with cookies you just picked up in the store than to bake your own and only send a box every couple of months. I baked cookies occasionally, but I sent store bought ones much more often. Most important of all is to just keep those letters and boxes heading out to your loved one.

Recipes for some shippable yet surprisingly good cookies and snack items

## Molasses Crisps

*These cookies, despite their name, are more chewy than crisp. They are easy to make, they travel well, and they stand up to the heat. They are very good and were appreciated by all the soldiers and marines I sent them to.*

- 1½ cup butter or margarine
- 4 cups flour
- 4 tsp baking soda
- 1 tsp salt
- ½ cup dark molasses
- 2 tsp ground cinnamon
- 1 tsp ground cloves
- 1 tsp ground ginger
- 2½ cup granulated sugar
- 2 large eggs

Melt butter in large saucepan. Remove from heat. Let cool.

Sift flour with soda, salt, cinnamon, cloves, and ginger.

To the melted, cooled butter, add 2 cups of the sugar, molasses, and eggs. Beat well.

When smooth and thick, stir in the flour mixture, a cup at a time. When the dough is well mixed, cover and chill 2 hours or longer.

Preheat oven to 375°F. Roll dough into small balls, using about 1 to 1½ teaspoons of dough for each. Roll balls in the remaining ½ cup of sugar, and place 2 inches apart on ungreased cookie sheet. Bake about 10 minutes, until cookie is dark, golden brown. Remove from oven and let cool about 2 minutes before moving to wire rack.

The great thing is, you can make this dough and then bake a dozen or so at a time and keep the dough in the fridge for the next day. Fresh cookies every day!

# Texas Hot Peanuts

Heat 3 T olive oil and add 2 T crushed red pepper and 4 minced garlic cloves; then add 12 oz cocktail peanuts, 12 oz of Spanish peanuts. Stir for 5 min, remove from heat, sprinkle liberally with seasoned salt and chili powder. Drain on paper towels.

# Ranger Cookies

*I had this 35-year-old recipe for Ranger Cookies and it was already a family favorite, but I decided that since I was sending cookies to MPs, an MP cookie was also needed. So I created the MP Cookie recipe that follows, which turned out to be pretty good also.*

- 1 cup shortening
- 1 cup brown sugar
- 1 cup white sugar
- 2 eggs
- 2½ cups all purpose flour
- 1 tsp soda
- ½ tsp baking powder
- ½ tsp salt
- 1 tsp vanilla
- 2 cups corn flakes
- 1 cup coconut

Cream shortening and sugar. Add eggs and beat until creamy. Add vanilla. Sift together flour, soda, baking powder, and salt. Gradually add to creamed mixture. Stir in corn flakes and coconut.

Drop by spoonfuls on greased cookie sheets. Bake at 375°F for about 10 minutes.

# MP Cookies

*I used a chocolate cookie recipe I had, and added some things I had available to create this recipe. It turned out to be pretty tasty, and the MPs liked having a cookie named for them.*

*(Really, I am not usually such a creative baker; I always follow the recipe to the letter. I think I was just inspired that day.)*

2 sticks margarine softened
$^3/_4$ cup sugar
$^2/_3$ cup brown sugar (packed)
1 tsp vanilla extract
Cream together until creamy.
Add 2 eggs and beat well.
Sift together in another bowl:
$2^1/_4$ cup all purpose flour
$^2/_3$ cup cocoa
1 tsp baking soda
$^1/_2$ tsp salt

Add the dry ingredients to the creamed mixture gradually, stirring well.

Stir in the following:

$1^1/_4$ cup white chocolate chips (or add the whole bag; who's counting?)
$^3/_4$ cup dried cherries (or cherry-flavored cranberries)
$^2/_3$ cup walnuts pieces

Bake at 350°F for about 10 to 11 minutes.

# Super Trail Mix

*This is a flexible recipe. You can adjust the ingredients to taste. Everything is healthy and good tasting though.*

Toss together the following ingredients:

2 cups banana chips (break these up into smaller pieces if they're too big)

$\frac{1}{2}$ cup raw sunflower seeds (substitute the salted kind if you want)

1 can cocktail peanuts

6 to 8 oz. candied pineapple chunks—you might want to cut these into smaller pieces, depending on their size.

2 cups dried cherries (can substitute dried cherry flavored cranberries)

Package separately: 8 oz. bag of M&Ms

The military person you send this to can then add the M&Ms and give the whole thing a stir or a shake, and it's ready to eat.

## Food Packaging

You might want to invest in one of those Seal-A-Meal kitchen appliances that seal food in more or less airtight plastic. I wrapped the homemade snacks I sent in plastic wrap, padded them well with paper towels or more plastic wrap, and then sealed them in food storage bags.

Once you have everything in the food storage bag, you can close the bag almost completely, and then use a straw to suck out any excess air. The more airtight you make the package, the better the cookies will survive the trip and the heat. I call this method "the poor man's seal-a-meal," and it does work.

You can also buy those disposable plastic tub containers and stack your cookies in there, being sure to put some paper towel or wax paper padding between them. Whatever method you use, just get the packaging as airtight and as padded as possible.

As a final note on packaging homemade goodies though, even if your best efforts fail and the cookies crumble, the guys and girls are still going to eat and enjoy the crumbs. Even when my packaging resulted in cookie crumbs, David always said, "We ate them anyway."

## Toiletries

Most of these things are available to military personnel in the PX now, even in war zones. It is sometimes difficult for them to actually get to the PX though, and even when they do, the lines can be long and the hours short. All of the soldiers and marines I sent packages to, appreciated receiving these items in the mail.

You know the brands your soldier prefers, and those may not be available in his location. Having a PX in a war zone is a giant step forward over previous military actions, but most soldiers still prefer receiving these things in CARE packages.

Send only unscented shampoos, lotions, and sun block. The scented kind attracts insects, which often abound in desert areas.

General Hygiene Needs:

- **Shampoo** (unscented)

- **Conditioner** (unscented)

- **Soap**

- **Body powder**  Make sure all powder has a sealed top. I also sealed the box in a separate food storage bag just make doubly sure nothing leaked out. It is not a good thing to have powder leaking out of a box in the mail. Security measures since the anthrax scare, especially in mail to military personnel, is tightened, and spilled powder of any kind is not a thing you want to be responsible for.

- **Deodorant** (unscented)

- **Moisturizer or body lotion**; hand lotion or cream (unscented)  Even tough guys need this stuff when the 13% humidity dries out their skin.

- **Waterless hand cleaner**  This is less a necessity than it was early in 2003 when the troops were constantly on the move, but it still comes in handy on patrol.

- **Toothpaste, Toothbrush, and Floss**  The aunt of one of the soldiers in David's platoon mentioned her "keep the soldiers supplied" project to her dentist, and he donated a box of toothbrushes—enough for the whole company. Toothbrushes need to be replaced every few months, and sometimes they get lost or dirty under even the best of conditions. It's better to have a spare when deployed, and this is something you can drop into a CARE package every month or so. Someone is bound to need it.

- **Mouthwash**  Small bottles that fit in a hygiene bag are good. They have to carry their hygiene items to the shower house and back to their rooms every time they shower.

- **Mouthwash strips**  A pack of these in a marine's or sailor's pocket can give him the boost of a clean mouth under the harshest of circumstances.

**Especially needed in the desert:**

- **Saline nasal spray**  North American nasal passages tend to dry out in extremely dry climates. This is one of the first requested items of soldiers after they arrive in Kuwait.

- **Visine**  Again, the blowing sand is hard on the eyes of anyone who isn't a Bedouin. This is a necessary item.

- **Lip balm or Chap Stick**  Helps fight chapped lips caused by blowing winds and dry heat.

- **Hard candy or throat lozenges**  Helps keep throat passages moist. It really is a constant battle, especially at first, keeping eyes, nose, and mouth moist. Every little effort helps.

First Aid Items:

- **Aspirin, ibuprofen, or Tylenol in individual packs**
  The medics, who are always nearby, supply these things, yes, but then again, sometimes a person just has a headache and wants to take a couple of aspirin without feeling that he has to "go see the medic" to get them.

- **Vitamins**  They get no real milk in most parts of Iraq, and fresh fruit, vegetables, and eggs are rare. Just a one-a-day multivitamin can help to keep them fit and healthy; this lack of fresh food is going to last about a year, so vitamins could make all the difference. Calcium and iron supplements are also a good idea.

- **Band-Aid**s  Medics have these too, but if it's just a scratch, it's easier if you have your own.

- **Neosporin**  It couldn't hurt.

- **Insect repellent (unscented)**  Desert equals all kinds of bugs, especially sand fleas. This is a necessity.

- **Sun block (unscented)**  They really need this too. Not much shade in the desert.

Foot care items. (Very important):

- **Moleskin**

- **Foot powder**  Gold Bond in the blue can is best. This was one of the most requested items. Foot powder, extra socks, everything for foot care comes in very handy for people who wear boots up to 18 hours a day, sometimes even longer when they're on a mission.

- **Insoles**

- **Foot soak**

- **Nail clippers**

- **Loofah**

- **Pumice stone**

- **Emery boards**

All military personnel must take extra care of their feet, even if they're not in the infantry. Be sure to send all these items often.

Shaving stuff for men and women:

- **Razors**
- **Shaving cream or gel**

They have electricity now, and electric shavers if they want them. Bear in mind the needs of your particular soldier, and keep him supplied with his particular shaving needs.

Feminine hygiene needs:

- **Tampons and Pads**
- **Feminine hygiene spray**
- **Panty liners**
- **Midol**
- **Individually packed facial gels**  The cooling kind is especially nice after hours spent in the heat of the Middle East or Africa.

# Especially Good for the Hot, Dry Climate

If the temperature is 120 in the shade, wouldn't a nice glass of iced tea taste good? They are well supplied with bottled water. All they need is a teabag to drop in one of those bottles and to let it sit in the sun for an hour or so. Some sugar packets or artificial sweetener to sweeten it, and they can then either refrigerate it or pour it over ice. I sent a gallon jug, teabags, and sugar, so David could make tea in large quantities. The jug I sent was glass, but plastic would be lighter and cost less to ship and would work just as well. This is much better than the instant stuff served by most military cooks. To a real tea drinker, even the bottled stuff isn't quite so primo as making your own.

Squirt guns, kiddie pools, and water balloons are all lots of fun. It may or may not be permissible or convenient, but you can send it anyway. If they can't use such items, they probably know someone they can give them to.

## Useful Housekeeping Items

When your soldier leaves for deployment, his commander will give him a list of supplies that he is responsible for providing for himself. He'll also have some personal belongings that he wants to take with him. And he'll have limited space in which to pack all these things. When he arrives, he's likely to begin immediately requesting things he either forgot or didn't have room for or discovers after his arrival that he could use. Even the commander can't anticipate all the needs of his troops, and this is where your regular CARE packages come in handy. It was easy at first to find things to send because there were lots of housekeeping items that David discovered he needed.

When David arrived at Camp Lima, his first duty station near Karbala, he discovered that there were no lights in the camp at all, the latrine was a long walk from where he lived and worked, and the nights were very dark. He didn't have a flashlight at his disposal (he had to keep his in his truck), so he had to borrow one every time he made that trek to the bathroom. Sometimes he couldn't find one, and there were a couple of times when he literally ran into people on the way because it was so dark, or he got inside the toilet and couldn't really see—not a good thing when you're sharing toilet facilities with a few dozen people. He sent out a desperate plea for a penlight. He described the conditions rather graphically, and I thought to also include some disinfectant wipes for cleaning the seat.

Someone told me early on, "Pretend you're going on a year-long camping trip. Think of some of the things you might need." Consider the following list of items. Don't send it just because it's on this list though. You or your soldier may think of items that aren't included here, and some of these things might not be needed by your soldier.

With that in mind, here's another list of simple housekeeping items your soldier or marine might need:

- **Good toilet paper** Early in 2003, this was on every list. I sent it a few times until David told me to stop. Toilet paper is readily available now so I would not send it unless your soldier prefers, would appreciate, or requests a particular brand.

- **Baby Wipes or Wet Ones in individual packets** These have many uses and are often requested. Send them. Look for unscented, antibacterial ones.

- **Phone Cards** You have to make sure the phone card you buy is good for international calls. David was able to buy these in the PX, so he could choose the one he needed, and the price was reasonable. It is good to buy the "rechargeable" kind too. Check out https://thor.aafes.com/scs/default.aspx for about the best phone card deal around for soldiers.

- **Sweat wicking socks and underwear**

- **Black Socks** Cotton-Long to wear with boots (Tube Socks).

- **Kleenex** Small pocket packs are good for carrying on patrol.

- **Q-tips** For personal hygiene and many other uses.

- **Wash cloths** In this case, quantity is preferred over quality. Buy a package of 10 or 12 for about $3.00 at a discount store. Wash them before sending them. These come in handy in the shower of course, but the cheap ones are also nice to use for cleaning weapons and equipment, and nobody has to feel any guilt when they just toss them away afterward.

- **Towels**  The bigger and fluffier, the better. Don't skimp on the cost of these. Be sure to wash them before you pack them though; they'll be ready to use right out of the box.

- **Hygiene bags**  If he didn't take one with him. All those travel shower equipment things are good to have. Soap on a rope, plastic soap dishes and toothbrush holders. Mesh bags for holding shower supplies or better yet, one of those that unfolds in the shower and hangs over the shower head.

- **Fly swatters**  It's insect heaven, so fly swatters and insect spray come in handy.

- **Back scratchers and bath brushes**  Useful in a dry climate.

- **Duct tape**  Comes in handy for a variety of uses.

- **Super glue**  Why not? It may be needed to repair something critical.

- **Sewing kits**

- **Safety pins**

- **Scissors**

- **Velcro**

- **Clorox wipes**  See the preceding section about the toilets at Camp Lima.

- **Mini mag lites**

- **Batteries**  Keep a list of all the electronic equipment you've sent or that your soldier took with him and know the size batteries required. Do NOT send electronic equipment with the batteries in place. A toy or game could be turned on accidentally during transit and cause a bomb scare. Pack the batteries separately. Pad them well so that corrosive acid doesn't have an opportunity to leak out and damage the contents of your box or others nearby.

- **Stick-up tap lights**   These are useful in many places, for instance, latrines that have no lights, over desks where light is scarce, on the bottom of the top bunk or on the wall for reading in bed, anywhere a little extra light is needed.

- **Office supplies**, especially letter writing materials. Pens, paper, and envelopes. They don't need stamps though. Postage is free for deployed troops to mail letters.

- **Clear Packing Tape**   He might want to send something to you or want to send some of his belongings home instead of carrying them back with him when the deployment is over. Some tape will come in handy when he does.

# Entertainment Items

- **Books**   I often used paperback books as filler and packing material to pad the rest of the contents of a box. You can buy these cheap at garage sales and used book stores. I sent books I thought David would like and books I figured somebody in his vicinity might like.

  There is usually a day room or rec room where they have lots of board games, maybe a pool table or foosball table, a VCR and monitor. If one doesn't care for a book or magazine he receives, he usually takes it there to share with everyone. Someone is bound to appreciate pretty much any books you send.

- **Magazines** You can send these in CARE packages. You can also send a subscription to your soldier's favorite magazine. Again, these are shared.

- **Hometown newspaper subscriptions** A nice touch of home.

  I liked to pick up those free local magazines and weekly newspapers at the grocery store or at bookstores. Most communities have some kind of alternative news media, and the 19- to 25-year-olds who mostly comprise our deployed troops like reading them. These too make good padding in the boxes of goodies.

- **Crossword and word search puzzle books**

- **Crayons, markers, coloring books, construction paper** Sometimes they get creative or maybe would just like to create their own holiday decorations or cards. Better not send crayons during the really hot months though; they could melt in the heat. In any case, be sure you package each item separately in a Ziploc bag, especially anything that might melt at high temperatures.

- **Store bought or homemade holiday items**. Easter, Christmas, Fourth of July, these times become even more important when you're far from home. Make sure you send holiday items at least one month in advance. The mail still gets delayed, and this is one item you want to assure of a timely delivery.

- **Frisbees** The bendable kind you can stick in your pocket is convenient.

- **Nerf footballs and basketballs** An indoor basket to hang over a door and a Nerf basketball can provide a lot of fun for a bored soldier when it's too hot to jump around under a hoop outside.

- **Card games**  Those famous Saddam Hussein/Baath Party cards are probably about worn out by now, so a fresh deck might be welcome. You might also send Uno and other such card games.

- **Dice and dominoes**  These might not come readily to mind, but they can play all sorts of games with them.

- **Board games**  The travel kind ships well. Ask about these first though. I was about to send David a few board games when he told me the Army was building them a rec room and stocking it with all kinds of games.

- **CDs, DVDs**  Make sure your soldier has a way to play these. If he didn't take a CD or DVD player with him, he might appreciate one now. Most of the soldiers have PlayStations or Xboxes, so you should find out exactly what medium they're using before you send games and DVDs.

- **A laptop** is good for playing games too and for playing CDs; Internet connections in their rooms are starting to be more common. Company computers are available for e-mail and Net surfing, but your own personal computer in your room is a boon.

- **CDs or tapes with messages from family members, CDs of favorite local radio programs**  A recording of the morning drive time show from your city is a refreshing reminder of home.

- **Letters and Pictures and Cards**  This category of items should have its own chapter. The most important thing you can send is a letter that he can take out and read again and again with news from home. Pictures are an exciting item to get too. Deployed troops like seeing friends and family members, special events, and holidays. They like knowing that you thought of them and took pictures to send them.

■ **Drawings and Letters from Children**  David's cousin sent him letters that she wrote from her daughter Kayleigh, who was about six months old when David left. She included pictures and wrote the letters as if Kayleigh were writing to him, telling him about her first words, her first steps, and favorite toys. He wrote back to Kayleigh in the same vein.

■ A friend of the family made a DVD of her daughter's third-grade class in which she interviewed the children, asking them simple questions, like "How far do you think it is to Iraq?" and then taped their responses. The soldiers were entertained and touched by the kids' ideas about the world, and the children enjoyed making the DVD.

■ **Gameboys**  These are handy and portable.

Sometimes I sent silly stuff like bubbles or pinwheels. I found that there was a great appreciation for the kiddy kinds of toys like this. Bubbles are fun and boredom-relieving, but they don't present much of an intellectual challenge. And sometimes the troops are not necessarily looking for a mental exercise, just a fun activity.

Maybe this is considered a toy, and maybe it comes under the "Candy" heading, but one of the most appreciated things I sent was also the most inexpensive. I was shopping one day and ran across some of that old fashioned "penny" candy. Little wax pop bottles filled with sweetened syrup, Necco wafers, candy necklaces, big red wax lips, wax teeth, and other reminders of being seven years old. I bought a bunch of it and put it in the next CARE package. David shared it, and later when I talked to him on the phone, I heard his team members in the background saying, "Thanks, Mom. Those were cool."

Let your imagination run wild. Walk the aisles of a toy department, grocery store, or department store looking for fun and unique things that will remind your deployed loved one of home. The toys of their childhood are some of the most fun and comforting things they'll receive from you.

## Miscellaneous Handy Items and Advice

- **Wrap around sunglasses**  These are most necessary in the sunny Middle East.

- **Detergent** is on some of the older lists, but it's probably no longer necessary. Don't send it unless it's requested.

- **Disposable cameras**  I took the camera to the post office with a padded mailer, had them weighed together, and bought enough stamps to cover the postage. Soldiers can mail letters free, but they have to pay postage on packages. I sent the camera. David took the pictures and sent the camera back to me in the mailer I sent him. I got the film developed. Then I sent copies of the pictures back to him so he could tell me who's who. It was a bit of a procedure, and it's better if you're able to use a digital camera and post the pictures on a free Web site or even e-mail them. But if no digital camera is available to your deployed service member, try the disposable camera method.

Take a trip to a sporting goods store and get more ideas: ice packs that get cold after you smush them (they could stick these in their pockets or inside their shirts for a refreshing cool down in the heat), freeze-dried food, all sorts of great things.

Ask questions about what your soldier and the people around him need. You might assume he has a bed because he has a room, but part of their training seems to be to adapt to whatever conditions they find themselves living in, so they aren't often ones to complain about personal needs. I sent David an egg crate mattress pad when he mentioned that he was sleeping on a cot with no mattress. I also sent him a pillow and some good quality sheets. This inspired him to fashion a mattress frame from a piece of plywood. He said that for the first time since he'd been there, his roommate reported to him that he snored. Later they got real beds, but the mattress pad still added to his comfort, and the pillow was a great gift. Wait until you're sure your soldier will be staying in one place for a while though before you send very much "housekeeping" stuff. If they have to move, they might not be able to take such items with them.

Some people sent soft drinks in cans. And some people sent alcoholic beverages, pork products, and porn—all strictly forbidden, but still certainly appreciated by the troops. I'm not suggesting that you do or don't. If you do, you'll have to lie to the postal clerk, but I'm sure she's been lied to before.

## Most Requested Items

I polled several family members of deployed troops and asked what they had sent that was most appreciated. I also asked some soldiers and a former Air Force woman what they liked getting. Here, in no particular order, are some of their responses:

- Candy, T-shirts, gadgets, new toys that they're missing out on by not being in the U.S.

- Freezer Pops, suckers, hard candy, chewy candy, gum, beef jerky, cookies, Ramen Noodles, tuna in the bag, chocolate-coated pretzels, chips, Crunch and Munch, microwave popcorn, rubbing alcohol, vitamins, peroxide, liquid soap, shampoo, deodorant, small zip lock sandwich bags, toothpaste, wet wipes, razor blades, electric shaver.

- Baby wipes, wrap around sunglasses, chap stick, and eye drops.

- Gold Bond powder, hot/cold packs activated by pressure. Extra white socks, extra underwear, DVDs, blank CDs to make music and videos, Gameboy or similar good hand-held game that passes the times. Letters from home—not just e-mails . . . best for lonely times to have something to read. Books to each soldier's taste. Saline nasal spray to wash away the sand. I sent a couple of soldiers two-way radios and they loved them.

# Tobacco Products

The number one, most appreciated item I sent to David all year though was his "chew." I, two years into my most recent "quit" attempt, went to the tobacco store once every two weeks and religiously sent him his Copenhagen. The tobacco products available to the men and women in Iraq are inferior, dried out, and not very good. They call them "Haji cigs" or "Haji chew." And, if they use tobacco, they'd rather have the American variety.

I know this might be a controversial topic. I know there are those who object to participating in or contributing to the tobacco industry or to someone's tobacco habit in any way. I know there are those who would prefer that their loved one quit all tobacco use. If your soldier or marine really wants to quit and asks for the nicotine patch or gum or lozenges, I think you should send what he asks for. But if he says, "Please send me some chew," well, I couldn't say no to that. I figured he had a lot more important things on his mind than quitting his nicotine habit. Tobacco use is a nasty and potentially deadly habit, and I wouldn't encourage anyone to take it up. I encourage those who use it to quit. But for that one year of living in harm's way from so many other sources,

I suspended my criticism and supported my soldier. He wanted "chew," so I sent it faithfully.

Amazingly, too, during that year of "living on Iraq time," I did not once relapse myself, not even while making regular trips to a store that sold only tobacco products. Follow your own conscience on this matter, but my conscience told me there are worse things in life than tobacco use; being shot at or having a roadside bomb placed in your path are just a couple of those worse things. A soldier who is far from home might find a bit of comfort in nicotine, and I am in no position to criticize or complain about it. (See the Sidebar in Chapter 6 for more on the very interesting topic of tobacco use by military personnel.)

## Items Pertaining to Faith

Although few want to talk about it, religion becomes more important when you're far from home and your life may be in danger. Send a Bible or a New Testament or a rosary or whatever is unique to your and your serviceman's religious beliefs. He may just throw it in a drawer and forget it, but if he does feel the need to get in touch with his religious beliefs, it is there for him. I know several who requested such materials, so send it if you are in doubt.

Do not, however, send bulk religious pamphlets. Those are not allowed in Muslim countries and are prohibited by Customs from being sent through the mail. We should respect the religion of the country we're trying to help.

# Conclusion

If I haven't said it yet, and I know I have, so I'll just repeat myself here: The most important thing you can send your deployed military family member is letters, cards with personal messages, pictures, CDs with messages from home, DVDs of family gatherings; it's love in a box or envelope, and it's something you can do that will be productive and helpful. The personal touch is what they miss and appreciate most. Food is good. Entertainment items help alleviate boredom. And personal items make your loved one more comfortable in a very uncomfortable place. Knowing that someone remembered them and cared enough to make that trip to the grocery store, the department store, and the post office, or even bake cookies and make snacks—that is priceless. Letters, just letters, were the single most requested item across the board.

Please understand also that you do this not just for your deployed troop, but for yourself as well. Having your own "job" to do in support of your loved one's deployment is some of the best therapy you can give yourself. I liked to think that my efforts helped to make their lives a bit easier and more interesting, and that in turn, that made them a bit happier and a bit more alert, and therefore, helped to ensure their safety. It didn't seem like such a stretch of the imagination either. I did not want anyone to feel abandoned or forgotten if I could help it.

# CHAPTER 3

# To the Post Office

```
FROM: David

DATE: September 23, 2004

TO: Mom

SUBJECT: Boxes

I got packages from Jess, and Celia, Dad, and Tina.
I'm getting short on chew now though; maybe you can
double up on one shipment and that will put me ahead
of the game for about two months. That's what
happened last time—Dad sent me a roll one time, and
you send them regular, and that put me ahead for a
long time.

By the way, I don't get a chance to write people
back when they send me a package, or maybe I'm just
too lazy to do it. Unless I can e-mail them, I don't
thank them for it, so if you could, thank them for
me and tell Dad to thank Tina and her friends for
me. Okay, I'll talk to you later and c-ya soon.
```

You have amassed the contents of the first box to be sent to your soldier in a war zone. You've done your research and found out what she needs and wants, and you have found a few "surprises" and treats to add to the enjoyment. Now all you have to do is find a box, pack the box, address the box, and take it to the post office. That actually could get to be quite an onerous task if you don't prepare for it. Not everyone has a mailing room set up in her house, but you now need to do just that. You'll need to make a few more purchases and find a spot to store everything for quick access, but once you get your mailing station set up, preparing your regular CARE package shipment will take only minutes each time.

# Get the Box

For free priority shipping supplies, go to www.usps.com, and enter the search term "shipping supplies" in the Search window near the top of the page.

You can also print an order form online or pick one up at the post office and then fax it to 1-800-270-6233 or order by phone at 1-800-610-8734. You can also just stop in your local post office and pick up all the boxes you want, but I liked the convenience of having them delivered to my door. They come in bundles of 25, and you'll easily use that many or more.

A #7 box worked best for my weekly shipments. It's about 12" x 12" x 8" and seems to hold just the right amount. If your local post office branch doesn't stock them (mine doesn't), you can order them online or by phone. Only priority or express mail boxes are free, so if you want to send parcel post, you will have to purchase your boxes or recycle used boxes.

# Good Ideas/Bad Ideas for Shipping

## Good Ideas:

Have several different sized boxes on hand as well as some envelopes for smaller shipments.

Put your own name and address inside each box along with that of the addressee. If the box gets torn or damaged and the contents spilled out, someone in the mail center may be able to repackage it and send it on its way. Without that information inside the box, if the outside is damaged, the contents will certainly never make it.

## Bad Ideas:

Don't cover a box in brown wrapping paper—the paper could be torn in handling and the address lost with the wrapping. Some people get the free priority boxes from the post office and then cover them with brown paper in order to ship parcel post. I don't recommend this, but if you decide to try it, be sure to put a mail sticker on the box itself, inside the wrapping. Then if the wrapping paper is destroyed, the box will still have an address on it.

Don't tie boxes with twine—the string can get caught in mail handling machines.

I also got some address labels preprinted with my return address. These weren't available when I ordered online, but when I called the 800 number, the person I spoke with asked if I wanted preprinted labels, and just having my return address printed on the label was a wonderful time saver. Each time you send a box, you will have to hand write the address information three times, once on the box or mailing label and twice on the customs form. Having one small part preprinted is a welcome time saver.

Before I discovered that the post office supplies free priority boxes and labels, I spent a few dollars on the purchase of strong, secure boxes. Whether you take advantage of the post office's generosity or not, make sure the box you use is strong and able to withstand a lot of tossing about. It should have little or no extra printing on it.

If using a recycled box, be sure to:

- Remove all former packing labels and address information.

- Remove all bar codes.

- Mark through or cover with stickers any brand names/commercial information that may be stamped on the box.

Mailing your packages by Priority Mail costs a bit more than sending them parcel post, and the priority distinction really only applies as long as the box is in the hands of the United States Post Office. When the box is handed over to the military mail system, technically, the priority designation no longer applies. However, priority means your mail will reach the APO or FPO it must be routed through in two to three days, while parcel post can take a week. Since new, strong boxes cost $2 to $3 each, and in most cases, the price difference between parcel post and priority is around $2 to $3, it seems better all round to take advantage of the free box and use the money you save on the box to mail the package by Priority Mail.

# Do/Do Nots of Packages

**Do** make sure to allow plenty of time for packages to arrive for holidays, birthdays, anniversaries, and other special dates. Normal shipping time to the Middle East is about two weeks for a priority box, a bit shorter for letters, and a bit longer for parcel post packages. The time can be longer at Christmas, or it can be increased by the simple logistics of fighting a war, by hostilities, or even bad weather, such as dust storms. If you want to be sure a package arrives before a certain date, I would send it a month in advance of that date.

**Do** include a packing list in the top of each box. The addressee can then check the list and make sure nothing was removed during shipping. This never happened to anything I mailed, but I have heard many stories of items gone missing from boxes. A packing list lets the inspectors know that you are keeping track.

**Do** enclose each separate item in a strong Ziploc bag, especially if there's any chance it might leak. Leaking packages can be and are destroyed.

**Do** make sure your boxes are of a reasonable size. Various deployment zones have different requirements regarding size. Check the ZIP code listing for your military man or woman in the latest postal bulletin. In general, the larger the box, the longer it will take to get there, so better to send two smaller boxes than one big one.

**Do not** gift wrap anything. If a package is opened and inspected, your careful gift wrapping will be for nought. Use gift bags and tie loosely with ribbon.

You can check the price difference for the different services at the post office each time you mail a package, or you can go online before you leave home and determine what it will cost to mail your package. A couple of times during the year, I found the difference in price to be significant, so I opted for parcel post. If you're mailing books or other printed matter only and you don't care how fast it gets there, remember to take advantage of the book rate offered by the post office. Printed materials are less expensive to mail than other items. Usually, though, your CARE packages should contain a variety of items, so that will only rarely be the case.

## Other Supplies You Will Need

You will also need some good quality packing tape (not Scotch or masking tape), preferably in a dispenser for ease of use, an ink pen, and a supply of permanent markers. I kept duplicates of these supplies in my car as well because sometimes I'd need to stop and pick up one or two needed items on my way to the post office and then seal the box after I got there.

### TIP

Don't stint on the quality of the packing tape. Get the good stuff and get a sturdy dispenser. Wrestling with an unwieldy tape dispenser and tape that tears easily or that you can't find the end of is a frustration you don't need when you are mailing multiple packages each week.

# Pack the Box

It's a long way from the United States to most overseas deployment areas, but if you know how to pack that CARE package securely, every one of your packages will make it safely to your deployed family member. You need a few supplies, and you need to follow some simple procedures. This is easy once you've gathered your tools and know how to use them.

Keep all your supplies—boxes, tape, markers, address information—in one place. I set up a workstation on a six-foot table in my laundry room. That table was the permanent storage place for address labels, permanent markers, tape dispenser, and "filler" items such as paperback books. When I found something I wanted to send in the next shipment, it was placed on the table where I could find it when I was ready to pack the box.

## Secure Packaging Procedures

Following are the steps you need to take to pack a secure box and ensure that it arrives intact and is delivered to the person you intend it for:

### *Line the Box with a Trash Bag*

One of those smaller white ones works best, and it's reusable for them to store things in (or as a trash bag). Seal individual items in quart or gallon size Ziploc bags (again reusable).

Lots can happen to the stuff you send to deployed military loved ones over the course of the two weeks (or more) it could take your package to arrive. The bags help keep the contents of your box from spilling, but they also help protect their contents from stuff that might spill from other boxes. Nobody wants a PopTart that tastes like shaving lotion.

Put the addressee's name and address and your own inside the plastic trash bag. If a box is accidentally opened, this might help get the contents on to its intended receiver.

## Packing List

I also put a packing list in each box. If someone has to gather stuff up after it's been spilled, that might make it easier for them to know what goes in which box. I felt that it also discouraged pilferage because if the inspectors knew I was keeping track of the contents, they might be less likely to help themselves to tempting items in case they did open a box.

### NOTE

To expedite the creation of a weekly packing list, I created a Word document with David's name and address at the top, my own name and address and the date (just like a template for a letter). Each week I pulled up the template, changed the date, and added the contents of that week's box. I also appended a short personal note just so he'd have something interesting to read. I tucked this into the top of the plastic garbage bag just before I sealed it.

See the sidebar for a sample of the packing lists I created each week. The header can remain the same each time, so you only have to change the date and the contents list and add a cheerful note each time. Then just print out your list and tuck it inside the trash bag you used to line your box. Sometimes if I had lots of news to report, my packing list/letter ended up being two or three pages long.

April 27, 2004

TO:      Spc. David Boshears
          Identifying Military Address
          APO AE 09332

FROM:    Sandra Doell
          My Address
          Martinsville, IN 46151

Contents of this box:

Tuna and chicken

Club crackers—because I figure you might get tired of Ritz

Bread sticks and ranch dip for them

Charleston Chews and Junior Mints

Bowls, forks, knives, spoons

Mayo and jelly

Hard candy

Razor and extra blades

Shaving gel (I didn't risk getting the aerosol can type, and this was the only kind that wasn't aerosol, so let me know how it works.)

Foot care items: Gold Bond foot powder, foot soak, an emery board/file thingy for rubbing off the rough skin, moleskin for pressure points in boots, insoles for air circulation.

Rice Krispie squares (homemade)

Chew

A couple of big warrior angels

If there's room after I put in the chew, I'll add a couple of boxes of cereal or some books or whatever fits.

                    Love you,

                    Mom

## NOTE

I got the package ready, typed and signed the packing list/ letter, packed everything as well as I could, and then would often have to stop on the way to the post office to pick up some item (in this case, David's Copenhagen). I always carried a permanent marker, a pen, and some extra packing tape in my car. This way, I could add the items I had to purchase on the way to the post office, and then seal the box after it was completely packed. Planning ahead and keeping supplies where you'll need them eliminates a lot of frustration and wasted time.

## *More Packaging Tips*

Use newspapers, magazines, and paperback books as padding in each package. You can get paperback books almost anywhere—used book stores, yard sales, flea markets. They make better padding than bubble wrap or packing peanuts because they're useful after the box is unpacked.

Pack everything tightly. Use plenty of padding. Pack the box and shake it around a bit. If anything moves inside, rearrange the contents, and add more padding if necessary.

## *Addressing and Closing the Box*

Write the address on the box or mailing label using a permanent marker. If you use permanent marker and the box gets wet, the address won't wash away. Tape the box securely closed. Reinforce all seams with tape. Be sure to use packing tape, not Scotch or masking tape.

When completing the address label, you must show the rank, full name (with a middle name or initial) of the addressee, and PSC (postal service center) number, unit number, or ship name. The APO or FPO line corresponds to the city name in a regular address and AA, AE, or AP takes the place of the state name. Following that is a special number that corresponds to a ZIP Code.

## A Quick Mini-CARE Package

The cost of sending a box through the postal system is determined by weight. The average cost of my favorite #7 size box, filled with a variety of food and toiletry items and sent with priority status, was around $12 to $15. You do not, however, have to be that ambitious. The important thing is to make sure your service member receives regular mail.

One of the friends I polled before writing this chapter said that she often sent CARE packages in small envelopes for quick arrival. She says, "I used padded envelopes that were about 5 by 9 inches (I don't really know the measurements, but they were about half the size of a legal envelope). I would throw in…baby wipes, a small individually wrapped snack such as granola bar or Oreos and then add eye drops or deodorant and a quick letter. These usually cost about three or four dollars to send and got there in two weeks or less."

## The Really Easy Way

If you are too busy to shop, pack, and go to the post office, try the services at <u>www.shopping.com/xGS-military care package~NS-1~linkin id-3062100</u>

# USPS Rules and Questions

You must take your package to the post office yourself when mailing it to a war zone. The mailman won't pick it up, you can't ship it from one of those "box" stores in the mall, and you can't drop it in a box. If it's bigger than a regular or legal sized envelope, you must take it to the post office yourself and answer the questions asked by the postal clerk and complete a custom form.

Since the War on Terrorism began, we've seen the introduction of some security measures regarding mail that are sometimes troublesome but are designed with our safety and the safety of our deployed troops in mind. It is our duty as family members of military personnel to cooperate with these measures.

For complete details for what is allowed or not in the area of your service member's deployment, go to the USPS Web site and follow these instructions:

1. Type "Postal Bulletin" in the search engine.

2. Click on Postal Bulletin/View Issues.

3. Click on the most recent issue.

4. Click on either PDF or HTML beneath the current issue.

You will be able to navigate to the area that contains information about your area of interest. There is a table on the left side of the page which lists all APO/FPO area codes with corresponding restrictions.

General restrictions that apply to Iraq, Afghanistan, and other Middle Eastern areas are:

- Mail addressed to "Any Servicemember," or similar wording such as "Any Soldier," "Sailor," "Airman," or "Marine"; "Military Mail"; etc., is prohibited. Mail must be addressed to an individual or job title such as "Commander," "Commanding Officer," etc.

- PS Form 2976-A is required for all mail weighing 16 ounces or more. In addition, mailers must properly complete required customs documentation when mailing any potentially dutiable mail addressed to an APO or FPO regardless of weight.

- PS Form 2976 or 2976-A is required. Articles are liable for customs duty and/or purchase tax unless they are bona fide gifts intended for use by military personnel or their dependents. When the contents of a parcel meet these requirements, the mailer must endorse the customs form, "Certified to be a bona fide gift, personal effects, or items for personal use of military personnel and dependents," under the heading, Description of Contents.

- Obscene articles, prints, paintings, cards, films, videotapes, etc., and horror comics and matrices are prohibited.

- Any matter depicting nude or seminude persons, pornographic or sexual items, or nonauthorized political materials is prohibited. Although religious materials contrary to the Islamic faith are prohibited in bulk quantities, items for the personal use of the addressee are permissible.

- Firearms of any type are prohibited in all classes of mail.

- Pork or pork by-products are prohibited.

- Fruits, animals, and living plants are prohibited.

- All alcoholic beverages are prohibited.

- Materials used in the production of alcoholic beverages (distilling material, hops, malts, yeast, etc.) are prohibited.

Check the restrictions that correspond to your service member's APO or FPO five-digit address code (the ZIP code). Some addresses allow you to send tobacco products and some do not. The preceding list includes mail restrictions for most Muslim countries.

You will be asked several questions by the postal clerk who accepts your package at the post office. These questions change occasionally, but they generally correspond to the list included here. I found that very often I knew more about the mailing restrictions than the postal clerk did. No pork. No alcohol. No pornography. No guns. That pretty much covers what you need to know. I don't think the "fruit" restriction refers to canned fruit. I was never questioned on that one, and I sent plenty of fruit cocktail.

## Customs Forms

You will need to complete one of two customs forms depending on where your package is being sent and its value: 2976 (Customs Form) and 2976-A (Customs Declaration and Dispatch Note). The smaller Form 2976 is generally used for boxes whose contents are valued at $400 or less. Over $400 in value requires the more detailed 2976-A. These are general rules, and they are subject to the whims of the post office computer. I was required to complete the 2976-A only one time. I was mailing identical boxes, one to an FPO and one to an APO, and the FPO address required the 2976-A. Expect to use the shorter form, but don't be surprised at an occasional unexpected difference.

Both forms are available at the post office. It saves time to pick up a supply of them and fill them out before you leave home. You can print them online at http://webapps.usps.com/customsforms/. You can also order an envelope with adhesive back for affixing Form 2976-A to your box.

Here's how to complete the 2976:

1.  Check the box for Gift.

2.  Describe the contents of the box:

    You don't have to list each individual item in the box. There really isn't room on the form. I usually just write something generic like:

    Toiletries, snacks, nonperishable foods

3.  You do have to put a dollar value on the contents.

4.  Sign and date the green side of the form.

5.  On the white side of the form, provide your name and address and the name and address of the soldier you're sending the box to. Also sign and date the white side of the form.

I usually just handed the customs form to the postal clerk who affixed it to the box in the proper place. Your local post office keeps the white side of the form, and the green side stays affixed to the box.

Completing the 2976-A form is similar, although there is room for more detail about the contents.

## Making Sure Your Package Arrives Safely

If you follow the packaging instructions here, you have done everything you need to do to ensure the safe arrival of your package at its destination. At the post office counter, the clerk will ask if you wish to insure your package. I only opted for insurance when I sent David his computer, PlayStation 2, and several CDs and DVDs shortly after his arrival in Iraq. Postal insurance covers your package only as long as it is in the hands of the U.S. Postal Service. Once it is handed over to the military in the war zone, the insurance is null. And that's where it's mostly likely to be pilfered, lost, or stolen—or even destroyed by a roadside bomb or mortar attack. Most of the time you'll be sending food and toiletries; my feeling was that I didn't need to insure that sort of thing. If it was lost, it was just lost. You have to do all you can do, and then trust to Fate to keep your package safe.

My packing list always included several angels to keep watch over the box's contents and to help protect my son when he opened it. It was a running theme of our correspondence that he needed to open the box and stand back so the angels could spread their wings. Just close the box and say a prayer.

## Contraband—What Is Restricted

You know the rules. You know the things that are restricted in the area where your loved one is. But it's her birthday, and you know she'd love a nice cold beer. Think about that. You can't ship it to her cold. Getting it cold after she gets it presents all sorts of chances for her to be caught with something that could get her in trouble. Or wouldn't your brother get a kick out of the latest Hustler, and what the heck, what are the chances you'd get caught?

I know some people who took chances with these things, and as far as I know, they got away with it. Just keep in mind that not following postal restrictions or lying to a postal clerk is a felony—a federal offense. You wouldn't want the FBI to make an example of you, would you? And really, it's not worth the trouble your loved one could get in if she gets caught with a disallowed item.

## APO/FPO

APO stands for Army/Air Force Post Office in New York City. All mail for deployed Army and Air Force personnel is routed through the APO where it is sorted, placed on available military transport and sent to the country designated by your ZIP code. Navy and Marine mail is routed through the FPO (Fleet Post Office) in San Francisco.

Depending on where you are sending your mail from, postal rates vary. From the Midwest to an FPO address costs a bit more than from the same location to an APO address. If you are on the West Coast, the FPO address will be less expensive.

# The Importance of Mail

Regular mail, which you can provide for your deployed loved one, is sometimes the only bright spot in a dreary existence. The landscape is the same, the clothes are the same, the menu in the de-fac is the same, but your letters and packages can supply a reminder that there is still a home and still people who long to see them again. Sending letters and packages is the single most important thing you can do. Don't let your enthusiasm for staying in contact in this way flag.

In all the wars of the previous century, from World War I through the Persian Gulf War, letters and mail from strangers as well as loved ones were welcome highlights in a soldier's or sailor's life. The tactics of the enemy in the War on Terrorism have precluded the possibility of letters from total strangers being delivered to your service person. It's up to you and the rest of her family and friends to keep her connected to life at home.

What do you say in all those letters? How much of life at home do you tell your military family member? Definitely keep the news upbeat. I think it is preferable to tell them everything that is happening, but even if bad things happen, as much as possible, you should give the impression that it's being handled. Downplay the negative but don't hide the truth.

How do you do that? It's all about spin. Instead of saying "Johnny flunked out of college and is now lying on the couch watching talk shows and soap operas all day," you could say, "Johnny is taking a break from school right now. I am enjoying spending more time with him, and we both wish that you could be here to share this little vacation with us." Try to keep the news from home upbeat. Being far from home in a situation that is alternately frightening and boring with little chance for enjoyment of the usual American pastimes is enough to deal with. At least the deployed troops need to maintain a positive memory of home, not one fraught with news of Uncle Frank's latest eviction notice or Aunt Mary's arrest for shoplifting. Spare them bad news they don't absolutely need to know.

## Creating a Mail Support Group

Early in the deployment of David's company, news began to leak back to the families of a few servicemen and women who did not receive any mail at all. Some of us got together and decided to make a concerted effort to end that problem. You aren't allowed to address mail to "Any Servicemember" now, but it is possible to ensure that everyone gets mail. We began to poll our own deployed family members for the names of anyone they noticed who did not get mail.

### Operation Adopt a Soldier

They responded, and so began a project (actually a couple of projects) we are all proud to have participated in. As our own soldiers sent us the names of their comrades who for one reason or another received little or no mail, we began by sending letters, cards, and packages to them ourselves. Soon the number of names became larger, and we started recruiting friends and family members to take a name and send some mail to a soldier. So began "Adopt a Soldier," a small personal effort to ensure that one group of soldiers in one place stayed well supplied with loving thoughts, snacks and goodies, and other supplies.

If you attempt such a project, do so keeping in mind the following caveats:

- You must have the service person's permission to give her address to anyone she doesn't know. Do not share this information lightly.

- Give the names and addresses of service people only to close friends and family members, people you know you can trust.

- Do not broadcast names and addresses to large groups of people, such as church groups. Especially, do not broadcast the information on a Web site or by e-mail.

This works better if it is kept on a small scale. There's more trust involved if the recipient of mail knows it came from his buddy's aunt or his sister's co-worker. As long as you don't set your sights too high, you can easily organize such an effort.

Check back with people to see how they're doing. Follow up and ask if they got a response. Sometimes a person with the best of intentions finds it too hard to actually follow through and send more than one or two letters or packages, so you may need to give that service person's name to more than one person. I found that I had more volunteers willing to adopt than I had names of soldiers anyway, so occasionally I just doubled up and gave one name to more than one person.

If you do find that church groups or schools want to participate, you don't have to actually give them the addresses. Just have them get their items together, write their letters, sign their cards, package up their boxes, and then hand everything over to you to address and mail. One church group also handed a friend of mine a check for over $200 to cover postage. People are amazingly generous and understanding. There is a real desire among the general population to support the troops deployed in the Middle East; often, it only takes one who knows the ropes (you) to give them a plan.

There are many Internet sites with Adopt-A-Soldier programs. The one at http://www.soldiersangels.org/heroes/index.php is very well organized. The site also includes a soldier's blog.

## Letters from Children

Another group of people who want to support the troops are schoolchildren. They enjoy writing letters as a class project, gathering donations to send Christmas packages, or organizing large-scale contribution efforts. Contact your local school. Or just ask the schoolchildren or teachers in your own circle of friends and relatives if anyone is interested. Actually, I found that people approached me about this, and I didn't have to do much to organize them. With David's permission and that of some of his buddies, I gave addresses to the children, and they wrote letters, made DVDs, and put together boxes of cookies and other treats.

## Books for Soldiers

This site, www.booksforsoldiers.com, was recommended to me by my cousin's wife. Mat was serving in the Marine Corps, deployed to Iraq during the same time my son, David, was there. Jess, Mat's wife, discovered this site, and wrote to request an underarmor shirt for Mat. One person sent him four of them (at a cost of $30 each). All the deployed soldiers have to do is ask. There are hundreds of people registered here waiting to send whatever your service person asks for, although they concentrate on books, DVDs, and relief supplies.

The site is legal because, even though you can't send mail to "any servicemember," the soldiers themselves register here, share their own addresses, and place their requests.

If you know people who want to contribute but don't necessarily want to send packages to an individual soldier, this site also accepts donations. You can use a PayPal account or send them a check.

This is one of the best Web sites around for people who want to support the troops. Visit the site, register to donate to the troops, register your own serviceperson and post his requests, or just read the mailing guidelines for ideas of your own. And tell all your friends to check it out.

## Other Organizations That Support the Troops

Here are some other places you can visit where you can get ideas for projects, find a serviceman to send mail to, register your own loved one to receive more mail, or just be inspired by the stories of what some Americans are doing to support the more than 1 million troops who are deployed around the world.

### Support Projects

Find links to other sites and get ideas for support projects: http://www.americasupportsyou.mil/. You'll find links here to the following Web sites and dozens of others where you can get ideas for projects of your own or participate in ongoing support efforts for our troops.

### Frequent Flyer Miles

Donate frequent flyer miles here: http://www.fisherhouse.org/programs/heroMiles.shtml

### Helpful Hints

This site has many helpful hints and ideas for what to send to deployed troops: http://www.marinemomsonline.net/hints.html

### Prepaid Calling Cards

You can send a prepaid calling card from this site:
https://thor.aafes.com/scs/default.aspx.

### Blue Star Mothers

Blue Star Mothers is an organization dating back to World War II, which is enjoying a comeback during the present conflict. They have lots of projects going on all in support of our troops. Check them out at http://www.bluestarmothers.org/

### Help for Families and Dependents

To help military families and dependents, check this Web site: http://www.unmetneeds.com/

### Help for Wounded Military Personnel

Check here for ways to support and help our wounded military personnel: http://www.mcleanpost270.org/oifoef.htm

# Christmas: The Most Special Time for Mail

With the help of our rear detachment commander and the organization skills of Robin Vaughan, one of the mothers of a soldier in the 66th MP Company, and after the success of our Adopt-A-Soldier Program, the mothers, aunts, wives, and other family members of the 66th, launched an ambitious program for Christmas. We set about to make sure that each of the 200 soldiers in the company received a special Christmas package. This kind of effort requires planning ahead; we actually began making plans early in the summer.

As Christmas drew nearer, we updated lists, made plans, and set up special "adoption" procedures for all the soldiers. There were 10 participants, and each of us volunteered to send packages or make sure packages were sent to as many soldiers as we felt we could handle. Robin was the liaison with the rear detachment and the organizer of the project. She got a list of all the soldiers in the company, put that together with the number each of us volunteered to adopt, and matched us up with our group. We all recruited our friends, families, and church groups, and so began a very ambitious project.

Each soldier in the company received a special Christmas Angel package with a couple of nice, fun gifts, lots of Christmas treats and candy, cards, ornaments, and other seasonal goodies, all enclosed in holiday bags and tied with ribbon.

This project was one of the most rewarding of the year of deployment, and it certainly served to give us all a sense of doing what we could to help with morale. Christmas is a hard time for the service people and their family members. Everyone wants to come home for Christmas, but the next best thing is to have home delivered to you in the form of gifts from home. If you don't bake cookies any other time of the year, the holiday season is the time to make that special effort. Do it for your deployed service person, and do it for yourself.

One thing to remember at Christmas time and on birthdays and other holidays is that you should not gift wrap items you send. In case the box is inspected by customs, the gift wrap will be destroyed. We found the best way to handle this roadblock was to buy gift bags, put each item in a bag, and tie it with ribbon. You could also use holiday tins and gift boxes. Wrapping paper is a no-no, but other holiday packaging is acceptable.

Above all, check with the post office at Christmastime for the latest mailing dates. For parcel post, the last day you can send mail and still be assured of delivery before December 25 is usually mid-November. For priority, it's usually one day during the last week in November. You already know about Christmas mailing dates, but you'll need to check even further and plan far ahead to ensure delivery of holiday packages to deployed troops. For all holidays and birthdays, I recommend getting the boxes with special presents out about a month in advance. The normal shipping time to the Middle East is about two weeks, but that can be longer depending on conditions—weather conditions and "state of the war" conditions. Sometimes hostilities have increased and mail is delayed or lost for reasons beyond the control of those whose job it is to deliver it.

# Conclusion

With just a little forethought you can make regular mail a part of your own survival tactics for this year. Better to embrace a project wholeheartedly and become a part of the deployment than to stick your head in the sand and pretend everything is fine. You are concerned about your deployed family member's wellbeing, so do something constructive, something that helps her and provides you with an outlet for your concern. Better to work than to worry.

Go a step further and organize others to help with mail and CARE package projects. Adopt service people who need to receive packages from home. Do a little research or follow some of the links provided in this chapter, and find programs that are already set up to make supporting the deployed troops easy for everyone to do.

## PART II

# Practical Matters

The advice in this part of the book centers on practical things you can do that will help you keep track of what the world is like for your loved one, what's going on and how it affects him. There's also advice that will simply make bill paying and day-to-day life easier for you and for your deployed relative or friend. Someone is going to have to take care of these matters for each service member who is deployed. For the most part, they are independent, of course, and take care of themselves. Most of the things they can't handle themselves are handled by their branch of the service, but there are some personal, practical things they'll need help with.

The focus here is mostly on one adult trying to take care of business matters for another (single) adult. The military helps spouses and dependents, and it does what it can for single soldiers; however, there are just some personal matters that your loved one would probably rather have a family member handle.

We'll also touch upon some matters that you probably thought you'd not be discussing with your adult child. Now though, your thoughts are turning to matters of life, death, wills, and what will I do if . . .

Writing checks, maintaining a home, looking after pets, just knowing that his interests back home are being watched over by someone he trusts are all invaluable in supporting a loved one who is deployed. These are some of the things that will be covered in Chapter 4, along with touching upon those serious matters that we sometimes find hard to discuss.

In Chapter 5, you will learn about some things you can buy or do that will make it easier for you to pinpoint the location of your loved one, know whether he's relatively safe, and help you understand some of the communications you might receive from the military while he is away.

# To Do Before Deployment

From: David

Date: Saturday, August 7, 2004

To: Mom

Subject: Re: Fixin' to leave for the Weekend

Yeah, I'll try to stay out of ambushes and things
like that when I can. I need you to do something for
me, I tried to do it myself, but the order wouldn't
go through because I don't know why. I need you to
go to www.rangerjoe.com, and buy me four pairs of XL
p.t. shorts. They will be black and say "ARMY" on
them. You will see a picture of a guy wearing a p.t.
uniform, he'll have on a gray Army shirt, and black
Army shorts. You can click on "Buy" next to the
picture and have them shipped to me. But I think
you'll have to use your credit card, and then get
your money back out of my account by writing a check
or whatever. I went to do my laundry, and somebody
stole all but one p.t. uniform. So I've been doing
p.t. and washing my uniform about every four days,
It's not too bad, but I don't like putting on the
same uniform that I sweated in the day before and the
day before that. All right, we are getting ready to
leave Baghdad today, so I'll talk to you later and
c-ya soon.

*Sandy Doell* wrote:

We're about to walk out the door for the weekend. Going camping. But we have Dave's Blackberry so I can still check my e-mail.

Speaking of leaving: Ft. Lewis calls once a month. The last time they called, last week, the private asked me to notify them if we went on vacation or moved or anything. I suppose weekends don't really count, so I'm not telling them that we're leaving today. They must have tried to contact people, and found them gone or their phone disconnected or something.

I got your pictures back just now. They're all pretty good. You'll have to give me a rundown of who's who in them though. The ones of the damage to your truck turned out good too. I was sitting in the parking lot at the drugstore looking at them, thinking that now you've been shot at and missed, the only thing that remains is…well, you know.

Those will have to go with the pictures of your Bronco from the wreck when you were 20. The damage looks about as bad.

I love you. No more wrecks or ambushes, okay?

Later,

Mom

# Organize and Plan in Advance

Who is going to make sure your son's car payment is made on time while he's caught in a standoff with a rebel group and needs to fully concentrate on the job at hand? There will be times during the year when he has some very important things to do and the last thing he is able to think about is maintaining his credit or making sure his car has antifreeze for the winter.

If there's a spouse to take care of these matters in his absence, that's great. But what if he's single? What if he's single, owns a house, owns a vehicle, has a mortgage to keep up with and property taxes to pay? And a pet to look after? Who is going to be his point man back home? That's the first thing your family will need to decide—who will be the "go to" person while he's away.

I did most of the business things for David. We did some things right, but we did some things wrong too. Here I'll offer you the benefit of what we learned from our mistakes.

## That All Important List

In the weeks preceding your soldier's deployment, you both should keep a list of long term concerns, things that won't just sit there and wait until he's back home. A deployment can last anywhere from six months to over a year, sometimes he might be unreachable for weeks at a time, and there will be issues, especially for a single person, that must be dealt with right away by someone who can take charge. Once you've decided who will be taking charge of his affairs, you'll need to get down to business and figure out exactly what those affairs are and how you'll take care of them.

Often, your family member will be leaving from a military base in a different state from where you live, so you'll have to make some of these arrangements long distance. By now, you're probably accustomed to late night or early morning phone calls and requests to dig out old receipts or bank statements anyway.

You'll need lists of account numbers, contact information for banks and creditors, online bill paying and bank account usernames and passwords, possibly child care and pet care information—pediatrician and veterinarian contact information, permission to seek health care for a child, all the minutia of daily life—and more.

## The First Week—Getting Communications in Place

One thing you'll need early in the deployment is an address where you can send mail to your service member. If the commander knows exactly where they'll be living, this can be supplied up to a month before deployment. Or if they don't know until they get "in-country" where exactly they'll be going, you might have to wait a few weeks after their arrival to get an address. In most cases, you won't be able to pick up a phone and call your loved one, so you should make every effort to anticipate things that might arise early in the deployment and make plans to handle them. It may seem too simplistic to say this, but I'll say it anyway: make sure your soldier communicates to you his address as soon as it becomes available to him.

Meanwhile, he should have an e-mail address where you can send messages that he can read when he next can get to a computer. Travel from Ft. Lewis to Kuwait and then getting situated once there and finally having time to go to an Internet Café where he could check his e-mail took David almost a week. During that time, messages from family members, friends, and probably some spam were piling up in his Inbox. His time on the computer was limited by a charge per minute or by large numbers of people waiting in line for a limited number of computers. So if I had anything important to tell him about business, I tried to be as explicit as possible in the subject line of the e-mail. If it was business and something he needed to address, I would make the subject line "Read Me First!"

## Keeping Up with E-Mail

In the long run, e-mail is going to be your most reliable and fastest communication device. In most cases, you can't just pick up the phone and call your soldier or marine. Although you will welcome a phone call at any hour of the day and instant messaging is a wonderful "real time" communication device, e-mail is just going to serve your needs best. You can e-mail her, she can e-mail you, and messages will be waiting the next time you both log on, no matter what time zone you're in or what time of day you pick up those messages. With a few modern technological gadgets, you can access your e-mail and forward all your phone calls almost anywhere too.

### NOTE

It's a good idea to keep a list of topics you want to discuss with your loved one near the phone. When he calls at 4:00 a.m., you'll not be caught quite so off guard and forget things you wanted to ask or things you had to tell him. Just a word or two to jog your memory helps when you're trying to wake up fast and have a meaningful conversation.

My husband and I love to camp and usually we take at least two vacations of a week or longer each year; we try to go as far into the wilderness as our popup tent camper will take us. In the past, a phone call home assured us that everyone in our large family was fine. Last year was a little different, so we stayed fairly close to home, but we did manage to get in a few long, relatively worry-free, weekends, thanks to his Blackberry and the ability to forward phone calls to my cell phone.

# Business Affairs

Anyone who is gone from home for a year will need a bit of help with such things as mail, checking accounts, upkeep and maintenance of property, special care for such things as pets, electronic equipment, and musical instruments—to name just a few special concerns your service member might have. The military will help with most of this. What they won't do is pay her regular credit card payments for her, keep antifreeze in her car, and feed and care for her pets.

My advice here is short. Your service member needs to choose someone in her family or a very close friend and designate that person as a joint signator on her bank account. She needs to choose someone, possibly the same person, to have her power of attorney while she's away. Of course, the person who gets these jobs must be someone your service member knows she can trust with her money. Those are the two main things that need to be done from a business standpoint.

In fact, David did neither one. He gave me the username and password to his online banking information, he gave me a box of checks, he signed several of them, he gave me a list of his creditors, and I managed to maintain his business affairs for him. I did run into a few bumps in the road though because of this arrangement, and my advice to all about to be deployed service people is

- Add another trusted person's name to your bank account.

- Get a credit card for making online purchases.

- Sign a power of attorney, putting someone in charge of your business affairs.

## For Single Adults Being Deployed

Your single service member (or couples who deploy together) needs to appoint someone she trusts to handle all her business affairs while she's away. This can be a parent, a sibling, or a close friend; it just needs to be someone with good business sense and someone she trusts implicitly.

My cousins, Eric and Amy deployed to Iraq together in November 2003. They left a newly purchased house in Idaho and a very active dog named Molly. They also left vehicles, a house full of furniture, all their personal belongings. All needed some attention and maintenance over the next year that they were away. Molly was shipped to Eric's family in Indiana; the house was watched over by a trusted neighbor, and Amy's family could check on it occasionally when they drove over from Washington.

If you're leaving a spouse at home to handle joint banking accounts and continue the business of your home, you won't need the advice in this section quite so much. Still, it might serve to give you a checklist of things to think about before you go.

## Bank Accounts

Someone needs to check your bank account at least monthly. David just gave me his online banking username and password, and I checked to make sure deposits were being made on schedule by the Army and no suspicious debits were being made. I also had several checks that he had signed so when any unexpected debts or expenses came due, I could complete the check and mail it to the payee. I really can't stress enough that a soldier or sailor needs to choose someone to handle this job who is trustworthy and savvy enough to use good judgment before just writing checks or debiting an account.

Servicemembers, if you love and trust your younger sister in all things, but you know she's a bad credit risk, just don't even go there. Find someone else, maybe someone you love just a little less, but know won't be tempted to wreak havoc on your financial affairs. I heard several stories from soldiers and their families about wives or girlfriends who just couldn't handle that responsibility. Choose someone who doesn't need money for anything, who won't be tempted to "borrow" from you without mentioning it. The person you choose for this duty needs to be just as trustworthy as the guy who "has your back" in battle.

Family members, if your soldier assigns this responsibility to you, make sure you are above reproach in your handling of his affairs. I never paid anything without telling David beforehand. He authorized me to buy a few things for him, and I saved my receipts and reimbursed myself afterwards.

If David and I ever do this again, I will request that he add my name to his checking account as a signator. A few checks came to him over the course of the year and I had to deposit them for him. There were times when I had to pay a bill for him and then reimburse myself from his account. It would have been much easier to do this directly from his bank account. There were a couple of times when I had to explain that I wasn't David but I had his permission to handle his affairs. Somehow I made this work for us, but it would have been much easier if I had been a co-owner of his account and had power of attorney.

I paid his regular payments by debiting his account online. He used his own debit card at the PX when he wanted to buy something. If something needed to be done with a credit card or in cash, I simply made the purchase myself and then reimbursed myself from his account. I purchased the PT shorts he requested in the e-mail that begins this chapter online using my credit card—actually I had to call the people at Ranger Joe because I was having the shorts sent to a location whose address didn't seem to fit into their online form. Then I reimbursed myself from David's checking account. This is a perfect example of the unforeseen happening; who could have predicted his PT shorts would be stolen from a clothes dryer in Baghdad?

Regarding debit cards, it is never a good idea to use them to make purchases online. Your service member should be sure to acquire a credit card before she deploys. It is best to make all online purchases with a credit card, not a debit card. Using a debit card can give a thief access to your checking account. And credit card companies insure your purchases against theft or loss.

David had a problem replacing his PT shorts in the e-mail that introduces this chapter because he was trying to use his debit card, and a few companies (wisely) don't allow debit purchases online. I bought the PT shorts using my credit card, had them shipped directly to him, and then reimbursed myself from his checking account. We worked it out, but it would have been much easier if he had taken a credit card with him.

Again, at Christmas, David did some shopping, and one company in particular asked him to call them to verify his purchase. Since calling them was difficult from his location, he asked me to call them for him. When I did, they asked if I had his power of attorney. I did not, so they didn't want to talk to me. We worked that out too, but it would have been much easier had we done things in a strictly legal way with all the t's crossed and the i's dotted.

By the way, when you are handling someone else's business affairs for them, even if the company in question says they can't talk to you, that doesn't mean you can't talk to them. So you just say, "I understand that you can't discuss his affairs with me, but he wanted me to tell you this..." And then give them the information they need. It's a bit tricky, but it's something to keep in mind if you find yourself in that situation.

## Power of Attorney

Endowing someone at home with David's power of attorney did not occur to us before he deployed. Again, if I ever have to do this again, we'll visit an attorney and sign the papers to make someone in the family his legal representative. We made it through most of his one-year deployment, but then a few weeks before coming home, he decided to purchase an antique truck online through eBay. When he made arrangements to transfer the money, there was a one-week delay while the transfer account was set up. Again, I had to call the seller and explain the situation. Then, of course, David's homecoming was delayed a few days due to regular troop movement logistics, so he didn't strictly live up to the deal he made regarding pick-up and final payment for the truck either. It all worked out, but not before I made a couple of phone calls and worked out new payment arrangements with the seller—after the transfer account became active and I was able to transfer the first payment.

Even spouses need power of attorney to make purchases, lease apartments, apply for credit, or access some military services. This is something that Judge Advocate General (JAG) can help the service member with, but it needs to be done before he leaves the United States. In fact, it is a good idea to pay a visit to JAG for some free legal advice before the departure date. The military makes sure that your service member does some things, but it's going to be up to you and him to follow up on any individual arrangements that need to be made.

## Bill Paying

Having the name of a trusted family member added to a service member's checking account is something you should definitely consider doing. Over the course of a year, there will just be times when it's necessary to pay an unexpected bill, make a bank deposit, or start or stop an automatic withdrawal. David's affairs were quite simple, and we thought this wouldn't be necessary, but still situations arose when I wished that I could just legally write a check from his account. I would pay a bill from my own account, write myself a check from his account, and then deposit his check into my account. That's a lot of money moving and writing of checks when I could have just written one check from a joint account and been done.

If your service member doesn't feel comfortable leaving one person in charge of all his money, it is possible also to arrange ahead of time to have the bank transfer a small amount each month from his regular account into a smaller account he holds jointly with a family member. Then most of his money is still held securely in his name only, but funds are still available for another person to pay bills or make purchases for him.

# Money Matters and Enlisted People

The following is quoted from the Pentagon Federal Credit Union Foundation Web site at:

http://www.pentagonfoundation.org/. You can make a contribution, serve as an advisor, or learn more about financial recovery for military personnel there.

"Did you know that predatory payday lenders who target military personnel are scamming our troops, especially at the junior enlisted ranks? These loan schemes include pawnshops, rent-to-own and high interest credit cards. Payday loans are particularly onerous and can result in fees of $1,000 or more on a 6-month, $500 loan!

That's right, the brave men and women who join the armed forces to defend our freedoms are all too often ill equipped to deal with personal financial issues. They are pulled in by unscrupulous lenders who set up shop right outside military gates, luring unsuspecting service members with offers of easy short-term credit. Before long, the service member finds him or herself deeper and deeper in debt, unable to find a way out. Financial pressures can compromise fitness for duty, lead to a denial of security clearances and place tremendous stresses on families.

Personal financial problems exist throughout the junior enlisted ranks. Illustrative of this is the pervasiveness of financial predators who frequent military installations with offers of payday loans and other services which drain the military personnel of much needed cash.

Commanders observe that if a service member is having financial difficulties, s/he is not focused on meeting military responsibilities, thus compromising the overall combat effectiveness of the unit. Recent reports have estimated that over 60% of security clearances denied or revoked have been because of financial problems."

Seek out honest, trustworthy financial advice for your military loved one if you aren't capable of providing it yourself. Go to your personal bank and speak to an officer, or encourage your enlisted service member to seek out financial advice through his branch of the service. By all means, stay away from payday loans and pawn shops—oh, and lottery tickets are bad investment too!

## *Who You Trust with Your Belongings*

Even a single person who is young and just leaving home for the first time has probably amassed a lot of "stuff." TVs, DVD players, computers, cars, motorcycles, guns, fishing equipment, golf clubs, tennis racquets, CDs and DVDs, and thousands of dollars' worth of other sports and electronic equipment, not to mention pets and furniture. All of these things (except the pets) will be stored by the military for the duration of the deployment if your service member so chooses. What your service member decides to do with his belongings while he's away may depend on geography. If your home is not so far away from his regular duty station, it may not be so difficult to just have someone in his family store his belongings.

There may be some things that are so expensive and important that your service member doesn't want to entrust them to military storage. David collects rare and expensive guns and hunting equipment. He left that collection at home with his brother where he knew it would be safe and that Scott would take the guns out occasionally and clean them and even shoot them once in a while.

Pets are a special consideration. Not everyone is willing to take them for you, so again, this is where family comes to the rescue. My cousins, Eric and Amy, shipped their dog Molly all the way from Idaho to Indiana to stay with his family while they were away.

Children of single service members are another consideration. Their care is probably something you thought through long ago; then again, I'm sure some National Guard or Reserve parents never expected to be deployed overseas for a year at a time. Just make sure you set up temporary guardianship and that any medical or legal needs of those children can be handled by the person you leave in charge of them. I won't pretend to give advice about this very important issue because it is not something anyone in my family has had to deal with. Seek the advice of an attorney; talk to JAG lawyers about special considerations for single service members and their children. Make sure the children are left with someone who loves them as much as their parent loves them. And then give that person all the power they need to care for that child, including access to health insurance information, inoculation and health history, and a loving caring relationship with the child.

# Relationship Matters

Your relationship with your service member will be affected by her deployment. Now, before she leaves, it's time to talk about some things you never really considered talking about. It's difficult to discuss matters of life and death, serious matters of the heart and conscience, especially with one so young. You probably never considered making sure your 23-year-old nephew writes his will; you probably never thought of making sure someone has his power of attorney; these are subjects usually discussed when you're past middle age and beginning to think about the legacy you want to leave your children and grandchildren.

It goes against our nature to think of young people dying before their parents. By the way, I want to emphasize that it is not likely that your young service member will die or be wounded. So far, over 400,000 troops have served in Iraq alone (one estimate says almost a million). As of this writing, 2,276 have died in Iraq and another 258 in Afghanistan. Slightly fewer than 17,000 have been wounded in action. Approximately half of those wounded were returned to duty. This information, updated daily, is available at http://www.defenselink.mil/news/. Odds are your loved one will return to you in good shape. That said, you still have to face the fact that he's going to defend his country, he's going to a place where there are people who want to kill him, he's going to a place where there will be a bounty on his head. He's going with the best training in the world, the best equipment, and a group of people who are professional warriors, so don't worry too much about him. He knows what he's doing.

Expect the best. But before this deployment starts is the time to prepare for the worst. Prepare for it and then put it out of your mind—well—try to put it out of your mind.

## Saying "So long" with a Clear Conscience

Over the course of my son's deployment in Iraq, I met some wonderful people, families of other deployed troops. These strangers came together with a common bond, and we all shared many personal thoughts and emotions. I learned something from each one of them, more from some than others. I learned that we should not take anything for granted, that we need to say "I love you," and that we need to put other things into words also. If there is something on your mind, something that bothers you, something you have always wondered about or thought about, a misunderstanding of any kind, now is the time to bring it out into the open. Talk about the things you've never talked about before. Ask questions. If you need to say "I'm sorry" for something, now is the time to say it. Examine your heart and share what you find there.

Many of the young men and women heading off for a theater of war are in their late teens or early 20s, a time of upheaval in many lives. They are just finishing up the process of breaking away from parental authority; they may still be in the throes of a teenage rebellion. Romances are beginning and ending; life is already tumultuous for them. Ironically, many of the parents of these young people are also going through a big change: empty nest syndrome and difficulties with menopause contribute to communications problems. Having a child head off to college can be a gut-wrenching experience, but having one go to war is unimaginably difficult for some of us.

Don't let any of that stop you from saying, "I love you, I miss you, and I'll pray for you every day." I can't think of a circumstance in which you would ever regret having said these things, but I can think of many times when you will regret not having said them. Say what you feel. Say that you care. Say what needs saying.

The people who had the hardest time dealing with the deployment of a loved one, with the everyday detritus of life, were the ones who had something uncomfortable hanging over their heads, something left unsaid, unresolved. If you need to say "I'm sorry," now is the time to say it. Say "I love you." Say "I'm proud of you." Open your mouth and let those things out. Nothing in life is as important as loving and caring for your family and letting them know that you love and care for them.

## Special Farewell Gifts

Sometimes you want to express your love for your service member with a special gift or memento. Some of the things David treasured most were given to him by his family. Scott gave him a special hunting knife before he left. David kept that knife strapped to his waist every day he was gone. He told me once that it was his constant companion, the Ace up his sleeve that no enemy would be expecting; and he told me that he felt naked without that knife. Scott also gave David a bandana with the warrior's psalm imprinted on its camouflage background. He had everyone in the family sign that bandana, and we sent it to David after his arrival in Iraq. It was a nice touch from home and a reminder that his whole family was thinking about him and praying for him.

David also treasured a soldier's Bible given to him by his aunt and uncle. It was one of the first things he asked me to send to him after his arrival.

A cousin had David's name imprinted on a special dog tag with "Keep Him Safe" inscribed on the back. He wore that dog tag on a chain around his neck the whole time David was overseas.

These little rituals and special gifts are not necessary, but they are tangible evidence of family love and caring. So are pictures and letters. Service members do treasure significant items such as jewelry given on a special occasion, books, Bibles, and small trinkets. It doesn't have to be expensive, just thoughtful. It will give him something to hold onto when he's lonely or homesick.

One mother told me that when her son was home just prior to deployment and again when he had two weeks of R & R during the deployment, she wore his dog tags—so when he was in danger, he'd always have something with him that she had touched.

## Advice You Can Give—From the Heart

Talk about your concerns and those of your loved one. Really think about the things you've learned in your own life that fit this occasion. I remember telling David that it seemed to me that you had to be afraid before you could be called brave. Marching fearlessly into danger is not courage; it's foolhardy. Feeling fear and still doing what needs to be done—that's the definition of courage, I think. It pays to ponder these things at this time. It's not going to be the best time of your life, but it will certainly be a time of growth and learning. There are many positive character-building things that will happen over the next few months.

Several people told me about having a conversation with their son or daughter and advising them not to let themselves be taken alive. Probably the greatest fear any of us has in this circumstance is to think that our child will be tortured or beheaded or any of the other atrocious terrorist tactics used by the enemy. I think we all feel that way, but few of us can actually voice our thoughts. When you can speak about something, you demystify it, take away some of its power. So now is the time to say what you're thinking, even if it is to blurt out "Please come home to me alive."

One mother told me when her son called to tell her he had "put things in order," referring to his will and life insurance, she just said, "I know, Son. I'm glad you did that." She said her pat answer usually would have been, "Oh, we don't need to worry about that; nothing bad is going to happen." But this time she knew it was time to face up to the fact that something could happen, accept it, and continue living with the hope that it would not.

## Things You'd Rather Not Think About

I hinted at this earlier, and if you don't want to think about these things, that's okay. You'll be all right. In our case, one thing was mentioned, and it led to a conversation about other things. It was personal, it was private, and we both had tears in our eyes while we talked. But afterwards, I knew some things I didn't know before, and I knew more about what I should do if anything happened to my son. Again, have the conversation and then forget about it.

## A Will

Before she leaves the country, your service member will have met with a representative from JAG to put a will in effect, to name a beneficiary of military death benefits, and to handle any other legal affairs she might need help with. It is still a good idea for you to bring this subject up and get it out in the open. Just introduce the subject and give her the opportunity to say, "Oh, yeah, if anything should happen to me, the Marine Corps will contact you about my personal effects. My will spells out what you should do with my things." It doesn't have to be a long conversation, just mention it, and move on. Just knowing that a will exists, gives you a bit more peace of mind. It will be one less thing for you all to worry about in the coming months.

## Talking about "In the Event of . . ."

Whether you have this conversation is up to you, but before my son left, I asked, "Is there anything you would request if you were able to plan your funeral?" Short question—very hard to articulate. He said he'd like it to be as simple as possible, but that he had that all written into his will also.

Just ask. It will give you something to hark back to if it becomes necessary. Again, just have the discussion, keep it very short, and then get back to normal. There's really no need to wallow in fearing the worst, but you do have to give it a thought.

## Get Yourself a Passport

Here's another thing I didn't do. Consider. If your child is seriously wounded, she will be transported to Landstuhl Army Base in Germany. If she's unable to be transported to the United States for a  few weeks or months, aren't you going to want to go to Germany and be with her? Having a passport is just one thing you could accomplish beforehand that might simplify matters later on if it becomes necessary for you to travel.

# Resources

**National Military Family Association:**
http://www.nmfa.org/site/PageServer?pagename=reus_parents-famsupport
This is a group dedicated to the parents of single military service members. You'll learn who to contact in each branch of the military to join or form your own support group.

http://www.americasupportsyou.mil/
A site where you can find interesting stories and ideas for ways to support all the troops.

**Office of the Special Assistant for Military Deployments:**
http://deploymentlink.osd.mil/deploy/prep/prep_intro.shtml
This site offers information and assistance on issues concerning deployed troops—checklists of things to do before you leave, health advice, even advice about post-deployment issues.

# Conclusion

Many of the things you do in the weeks preceding deployment are going to be critical to your family's peace of mind over the coming year. Just knowing that you have made all the practical arrangements necessary and have taken care of the physical, business, and legal concerns of your service member means you don't have all those things to worry about. You've made arrangements to pay the bills, keep the house maintenance up to date, care for the children and pets, keep the oil changed in the vehicles, and take care of any unanticipated emergency financial needs. You've had the talks about life and death, you've cleared the air regarding any misunderstandings from the past, and all you have to focus on now is helping see your loved one through a long absence from home. In Chapter 5 you'll learn some simple measures you can take that will keep you feeling connected and comforted while he's away.

# Day-to-Day During Deployment

Note: The following e-mail exchange occurred between my cousin Carol and me early in April 2004. Her son Eric and daughter-in-law Amy were in Mosul at the time, while David was in Karbala. This exchange happened a short time after the bodies of four American contractors were mutilated and left hanging from a bridge overpass in Fallujah. The Mahdi Army was about to become active in Karbala and Najaf, and the summer was getting ready to heat up all over Iraq. David had been "incountry" about a month, and Eric and Amy had been there about three months. Carol and I were trying to help each other learn all we could about what to expect from the military and were just learning to pinpoint the areas where our children were living and working.

From: Carol

To: Sandy

Sent: Tuesday, April 6, 2004, 10:16 p.m.

Subject: RE: The Weekend

Yeah, the bad thing about the Army is that they don't care about family communication when they have a mission to fulfill. I know it's best that way but it's so frustrating. I remember that Eric was in the field when 9/11 happened and I was frantic to know he was safe. Amy was able to get a little information from her contacts, but it was pretty sparse and we were both kinda nervous. He didn't even know about it until a day or two later. Every time I hear the news, I thank God that the chaplain hasn't walked up my path...and pray for the families where he has.

My mother in law would probably like a map. I have one and so do my folks. You can mail it to me, and I'll explain the locations to her. It will be easier if I just take it to her and show her all the places. I have my map on the wall in the bedroom. No pins but I've highlighted Mosul, Karbala and Fallujah. Baghdad is pretty easy to see. I never did find the place where Eric and Amy were when they first arrived. And don't care now!

I'm torn between wanting to know more about the geography, etc. and wanting to bury my head in the sand! I guess I'm not a seeker of knowledge about this right now. I've even been deleting the FRG newsletters unread. Figure they won't tell me much more than I already know. Guess I should start reading them....

Keep the faith! Carol

From: Sandy

To: Carol

Sent: 4/5/04 9:23:42 AM

Subject: The Weekend

Well, I haven't heard anything from David all weekend. I figure they are either locked down pretty tight or are out patrolling, trying to keep the peace in Karbala. The last time he mentioned any of this, he said they were preparing for yet another major religious holiday with pilgrims flocking in from all over the place.

This morning I was wondering if perhaps some of his outfit had been called in to surround Fallujah, which apparently happened overnight. I don't know if there are enough Marines to do it, so they may have needed help. On the other hand, I know that where David is, they're short-handed and they have a mission of their own, so probably not. Wherever he is, I'm sure he's keeping his head down. It's just that sometimes I think keeping your head down may not be enough.

Anyway, I was going to ask: Would you or your mother-in-law like a map of Iraq? When I bought mine at Borders, I picked up two of them, thinking somebody else would like to have one, but so far nobody has expressed much interest. I could drop it in the mail if you want it.

I'm going to hang mine on the wall and stick pins in it where I know they are. I also bought a world map for good measure, so I can figure out a few more things—geography-wise. I've never really cared all that much about geography. Now I want details about a place half a world away.

The preceding three chapters of this book were all about things you can do for your deployed service member loved one. Those are things you need to do for him that can make both your lives more manageable and help keep him focused on the task at hand: staying safe in a hostile environment. The focus shifts with Chapter 5 though and throughout the rest of this book. All those things you learned to do well in Chapters 2, 3, and 4 (package cookies, provide needed supplies, make sure bills are paid on time, ensure emotional health going into this experience) serve a twofold purpose. They are not only practical things you can do for your service member, they also give you a sense of purpose, of doing something positive and practical instead of wringing your hands, worrying, and losing sleep.

In this chapter, we will begin to talk about things that serve only your peace of mind. You will wonder what it's like where he is, what kind of facilities he has access to. Is there air conditioning? A fitness center or gym? What's the food like? What's his work day like? Some of these are things you'll need to learn directly from your service member, but there's a lot you can find out about the place he's living on your own that will help you understand what life is like in "the sandbox." This won't necessarily improve conditions for your service member, but, used in conjunction with the other tools you'll learn about in this book, it will help to provide you with peace of mind. It will also give you a lot of inspiration for welcome CARE package items.

In this chapter, we're going to talk about geography, base camps, forward operating bases, climate, culture, and people. You'll learn how to quickly familiarize yourself with life in a part of the world we in Western society paid small attention to until a couple of years ago.

# Learn About the Place

The following Web sites and resources will help you towards a better understanding of the time zones, geography, terrain, and culture of the country your service member is calling home these days. You'll want to keep these resources handy for quick reference.

## Time

You can stay apprised of the current time anywhere in the world by checking the World Time Server at www.worldtimeserver.com. Scroll through the list of countries and cities on the left until you find the one of interest to you. Click on it, and voila! You know what time of day it is in your loved one's location. In fact, it might be tomorrow.

My friends and I referred often to "living on Iraqi time." When we in the United States were waking up in the morning, we knew that their workday was coming to a close in Iraq. If they had been out on patrol, they were probably back by now. If they had been able to get to a computer that day, maybe we had an e-mail waiting for us. And, of course, we wanted to check the news stories to see what had happened that day (while we slept here) on the other side of the world.

Bookmark the time server. You'll want to check it often.

## Weather

You'll want to know about the weather, of course. It's hot in the summer in Iraq and Afghanistan, hot and dusty in most places. Iraq has a fertile crescent of land between the Tigris and Euphrates Rivers. Afghanistan has some mountainous elevations. Both countries are susceptible to major dust storms. But did you know that some northern areas get snow during the winter? Korea is in a more northern area of the world than you might at first think. You might be surprised by the varying temperatures throughout the year in any of these countries.

It seems, for instance, that we simply think of Iraq as being hot, dusty, dry, and miserable. The truth is much more varied than that. We remember the dust storm during the invasion in 2003, but parts of Iraq in the north are mountainous, and parts border on the Persian Gulf.

Keep track of the weather anywhere in the world at weather.cnn.com/weather/. You'll find the current temperature, a five-day forecast, and satellite pictures of the country that concerns you.

# Maps

You can find lots of things on the Internet, but really good maps are not free for the printing. There are outlines of a country with major cities flagged, but that's about all you'll get by searching the Internet. Fairly decent ones are available at WorldAtlas.com and at cia.gov/cia/publications/factbook/geos. Both show borders and the locations of major cities, and the one at World Atlas gives some rudimentary topography coloring, and pictures each country on a world atlas as well, giving you a better idea of where its place is in the world.

Nothing I found on the Internet though gave me the detailed information I wanted. When I heard that a roadside bomb had exploded in Diyala Province, I wanted to know just where that was in relation to my family members, who were in Mosul, Hilla, and Najaf. I wanted to know where every small town mentioned in a news article was located, its proximity to larger towns that I did know the location of, and what kind of roads connected them all.

I actually found city maps of Karbala and Baghdad. Want to know where Haifa Street is in relation to Baghdad International Airport? There's a street map at mideastweb.org/baghdad2.htm that will show you. Just do a Google or Yahoo search for the words "map of Karbala," or "Najaf," or "Kabul," or whatever you want to see in detail. You'll find street maps, satellite images, and lots of information about the town of interest to you.

I wanted a wall map of the entire country though, one that showed the roads, elevations, the small towns, and where they were in relation to the larger ones, and I could not find that on the Internet. I found mine at Borders; it's published by Hammond, and I paid about $7 for it. I also bought a world map because I wanted to have a better idea of where Iraq was in relation to other Middle Eastern countries. When David got to go on a four-day R & R (rest and relaxation) trip to Qatar, I could look that up too and see where he was spending his time in relative safety from the rigors of the summer of '04 in Karbala, Najaf, Baghdad, Hilla, and Babylon.

Search Amazon.com for "road map of Iraq" or "road map of Afghanistan" and you'll find five or six other possibilities, most of them for less than $10. Buy a map like this; it will be the most helpful item in your arsenal of stress relievers.

I used that wall map of Iraq daily. It still hangs behind my desk, and when I see a story about something that happened in al Karmah, I might like to know just how far al Karmah is from Ramadi and if it's likely that someone patrolling in and around Ramadi might have been involved.

# A Lesson in Relative Geography

Americans are the worst people in the world for learning and understanding geography. The average man on the street can't tell you whether Korea is north or south of China. In fact, the average man on the street, unless he lives in one of those states, can't tell you whether Nebraska is north or south of Oklahoma. Most of us are content to know how to get around in our hometown and how to get on a plane to go anywhere that's more than a day's drive away. Beyond that, we just really don't care much.

You, of course, have steeped yourself in knowledge of Afghanistan, Korea, The Philippines, or wherever you loved one is headed. So now when friends and relatives do express an interest, how do you explain where he is to them? It is simple; all you have to do is relate the geography of the country where your loved one is to some geography that your friends and family are familiar with.

For instance, Baghdad is pretty much in the middle of Iraq. Mosul is about 200 miles north of Baghdad. Fallujah is about 40 miles west, Hilla is 30 miles south, and Najaf about 50 miles south.

I drew a very rough map of Iraq and another of Indiana, which happens to be the geography my family is most familiar with. Then I said, "Okay, Baghdad is like

Indianapolis; it's right in the middle." Fallujah is like Plainfield; it's a few miles west of Indianapolis. Mosul relates to South Bend because it's a good distance north." And so on. I found a place they were familiar with and then related it to where things were happening in Iraq.

This helped to set their minds at ease a bit because they had a better understanding then of where David was, so when they heard of violence taking place in Mosul, they knew he was far to the south of Mosul and not likely involved in that particular news story.

You can do this with your region too. Look at a map of your home state or region. Find a large city or landmark that you can relate to Baghdad in terms of size and importance in the area. Then find towns, cities, lakes, whatever landmark stands out and sort of superimpose that over a map of Iraq.

If you live in Texas, you could compare Austin to Baghdad, San Antonio to Karbala, Waco to Tikrit, and Dallas/Ft. Worth to Mosul. This takes some imagination and thought, but it really does help everyone to understand where your loved one is in relation to the news story of the day.

Of course, you can do this with all the other deployment locations in the world. Just relate the geography of the foreign land to geography that everyone in your area is familiar with. Let Atlanta be Kabul or Los Angeles be Seoul. If you put your imagination to work, you can understand better yourself and explain it to your friends and family.

Here are maps of Iraq and Indiana to scale.
This will give you some idea as to the size of
Iraq and the distances between cities.
Compare the distances in your own state.

## Globalsecurity.org

This is a very interesting and comprehensive Web site. Need to have rank explained to you? Medals and ribbons? Want to learn about the weapons your loved one so casually mentions carrying? All that and more is here. Just about any military question you have can be answered at www.globalsecurity.org.

Especially helpful to me was a listing of all the camps and bases in Iraq. I book-marked the page at www.globalsecurity.org/ military/facility/iraq.htm and visited there almost daily. Back up a level to www.globalsecurity.org/military/facility, and you can follow the links to a list of U.S. bases and camps anywhere in the world. This site tells you where each base, each camp, each fort, each outpost of our military is and provides a description of the town where it's located.

There is a list of all the military camps in the world, American and others, with descriptions of the surrounding countryside, the culture and history of the place where that camp is located. This was the most helpful Web page I ran across, and I highly recommend it to you. You will find the answers to almost all your questions here. You'll also find many satellite photos of those bases. I was surprised when I ran across this information because I actually thought a lot of it would be classified.

# Things You'll Want to Ask Your Service Member Loved One About

Some things, of course, you'll want to ask your loved one to tell you about. It's interesting to hear his perspective on the area you just read about or looked up on a map. Ask him about the people. Do the children they pass in the street wave at them, or do they throw rocks? I wanted to know all I could know about how

Scenes from
Iraq 2004

David was living. I asked for pictures of their rooms, the showers, the dining facility. I asked him to take his camera with him to eat and take a picture of his tray. Over the top curiosity? Maybe, but then again, it helps to know about these things. It helps to know the people he's working with and have a picture in your mind of his surroundings.

You will also want to know some of these things so you can ask intelligent questions and have meaningful conversations. Otherwise, all your conversations would be about things happening at home and just saying "I love you" and "I miss you." And dwelling too much on those things leads to tears and emotions you really can't afford to display very often. He doesn't need to deal with your emotions right now. He knows you miss him, and he misses you, but you need to find something to perk up the conversations when he calls or when you exchange e-mail. It just helps to have something concrete to talk about, to ask about, and to learn about from him. It also helps for you to be as informed as possible about the region. The next sections will point you to some resources that will increase your knowledge of places around the world.

## Geographical, Political, and Cultural Resources

Learning about the culture where your service member is stationed is the next best thing to being there. You want to be an informed supporter, not just a blindly worried relative. The more you know, the more secure you will feel, and the better support you can provide. Besides, it isn't just an idle saying that you should "know your enemy." The more you know, the more you'll be able to share with your service member; and who knows, perhaps he'll learn something from you that will help him interact with the citizens where he's living.

Here's a list of just some of the many books and resources available to you about some of the places we have deployed troops right now. The more you know, the less you worry, so read these and look for more.

## Islam and the Arab World

*Understanding Arabs: A Guide for Westerners (The Interact Series)* by Margaret K. Nydell, Intercultural Press, 2002

*What Everyone Needs to Know About Islam* by John L. Esposito, Oxford University Press, 2002

*Islam for Dummies* by Malcolm Clark, For Dummies, 2003

## Iraq

*The Complete Idiot's Guide To Understanding Iraq* by Joseph Tragert, Alpha, 2002

*Iraq: The Bradt Travel Guide* by Felicity Arbuthnot and Karen Dabrowska, Bradt Travel Guides, 2002

*Inside Iraq: The History, the People, and the Modern Conflicts of the World's Least Understood Land*, ed. John Miller, Aaron Kenedi, and David Rose, Marlowe & Co., 2003

*A History of Iraq* by Charles Tripp, Cambridge University Press, 2002

## Afghanistan

*The Sewing Circles of Herat: A Personal Voyage Through Afghanistan* by Christina Lamb, Perennial, 2004

*The Bookseller of Kabul* by Asne Seierstad, Little, Brown, 2003

*Afghanistan: A Short History of Its People and Politics* Martin Ewans, Perennial, 2002

*Afghanistan: A Military History from Alexander the Great to the Fall of the Taliban* by Stephen Tanner, Perseus Books Group, 2003

Search amazon.com for references on the country where your loved one will be stationed. Go to the library and look for books there. Information is available, and the more you know about the place and the people where he'll be spending his time, the less stressful the whole situation will be for you. You can also share some of that stress-reducing knowledge with your service member.

I read at some point that in Iraq the arm gesture we use that means "come here," to them means "go away." And vice versa. I shared this with David, and he said he would try it out when the occasion presented itself. Little things like that, little ways we can understand someone from so very different a culture, can mean all the difference sometimes in establishing peaceful exchanges with the citizens.

# Modern Communication

My grandmother was a "war mother" during World War II. Four of her six sons were in the military during the war, and I don't think I ever knew until last year what kind of torment that had to be for her. I have a diary she kept during that time, and the refrain "no letter today" is continuous on page after page. Occasionally, there would be a notation that she had a letter from one or the other of my uncles, and the joy almost jumps off the page at you.

Those "snail mail" letters are still important to servicemen, but we have many other communication devices at our fingertips these days. You can take advantage of all these methods so that not more than a day or two need pass before you hear directly from your serviceman or woman.

We do not have to endure the kind of pain my grandmother's generation suffered through those long war years. We have e-mail, instant messenger, international phone service, mid-deployment breaks, and a better understanding of the day-to-day circumstances of our loved ones. Following is an overview of the many devices and services available to you for staying in touch. Use them all. You will feel better every time you can communicate with your loved one in harm's way.

## E-Mail and Instant Messenger

Use your computer. Use it for research. Use it for daily news from the area where your loved one is. But most of all, use it to talk to him or her. Make sure before your service member leaves that he has set up an e-mail account that he can access from anywhere. Yahoo!, MSN, AOL, or any one of thousands of service providers can enhance your daily communication. In fact, it doesn't hurt to have a couple of these addresses; most of them are free.

E-mail is great because it is communication that does not require you both to be present. You can send an e-mail while he's asleep, and he can read and answer it while you're asleep. On the other hand, Instant Messenger (IM) services are wonderful for "real-time" conversations. There are several of these services too, and as long as you are a registered user of an Internet service provider, you can use their instant messenger service. Make sure you are both signed up with the same service. David and I used Yahoo Instant Messenger, and sometimes we talked almost daily. He enjoyed using this communication method with his brothers, uncles, and cousins too.

# Snail Mail

I think I may have said this before, but I'll just say it one more time: Nothing beats a letter you can hold in your hand, tuck into your helmet liner, take out and read while you're curled up on a rooftop or sitting quietly in a humvee waiting for someone to show up for a rendezvous. Letters are the best, maybe because it is a physical thing that you touched and that he can now hold and touch. People tend to speak from their hearts in letters more than they do in e-mail. Phone conversations can be short and often we don't actually say what we meant to say, but letters are the perfect form of communication during long separations. Use e-mail, talk often on the phone, instant message every day, but write letters too. Every box I sent to David while he was in Iraq came with a letter. He got pictures and postcards and notes and cards every time there was a mail call. No service member should have to sit through even one mail call without hearing his name. Send mail. Send it to your solder. Send it to others whose address comes your way. Write letters. Write as many letters as you have time to write.

# Phone calls—phone cards and cell phones

Phone calls, at this point in the state of most "hot" zones, are something you will just have to wait for your service member to initiate. We haven't reached that point of stabilization yet in most of these areas that will allow you to just pick up the phone and call your son, daughter, brother, sister, loved one, and say, "Hey, how's it going?"

When he calls you, he will be using either a government telephone or a calling card. Your caller ID will show "Georgia Call" or "Colorado Call" or some other such designation if he's using a calling card. If he's calling from a U.S. Government phone, your caller ID will show "U.S. Government." That can be frightening the first time it happens. Actually, I think it was frightening every time it happened, come to think of it.

You can, of course, send him phone cards in your letters and packages. They are welcome. Make sure the card is enabled for international calls. These are available at the post office, and I know you're going to be visiting the post office once a week, so pick them up there. We found it best for David to just buy one at the PX and then keep adding minutes onto it using his debit card. Whatever works best for your family is the way to go; just make sure your service member has a phone card in his pocket all the time. You never know when he may have a few extra minutes and a handy telephone.

Just before David left Iraq in early 2005, some soldiers were beginning to carry cell phones. They also were in the early stages in his area of being able to have Internet connections in their rooms. Communication is improving daily, and the availability of all these services just depends on your serviceman or woman's location. Just be aware that they are possibilities and ask about them.

## NOTE

My experience in deployments is limited to my son's and my three cousins' deployments to Iraq. Your loved one may be deployed to another country, such as Afghanistan, Korea, Colombia, or any number of "hot spots" around the world where the United States is involved in an active war, a peacekeeping effort, the drug war, or relief work after natural disasters. My techniques, however, are applicable no matter what country or area of the world you have developed a new and unexpected interest in.

## Telephone Advice

It goes without saying that you will not want to miss any phone calls from your service member who's deployed overseas. One of the worst feelings was to run out to the grocery store and return an hour later to see that David had called while I was out. What you want is continuous 24-hour availability, and that is hard to maintain for a whole year. You can come close though.

Make sure your deployed service member has a list of contact information for the entire family—at all times of day. If he should miss getting to talk to his mother, perhaps he can reach his grandmother or his uncle at work.

## NOTE

Before David left for Iraq, we had one of our big family gatherings, with all his parents, grandparents, uncles, aunts, cousins, and a few friends. I had purchased a small address book, and we passed it around and asked everyone to put in their home phone, cell phone, work phone, mailing address, e-mail address, every possible way they could be reached at any time. So he didn't have to work to gather all this information himself; there it was, all concise and in one place for him. Of course, he probably had most of it anyway, but it was a good thing to have it all in that one book. How many phone numbers and mailing addresses can you keep in your head at any given time? And how many do you think will stay there when you are in a stressful situation. That little phone number/address book came in handy quite often.

Following are some other tricks and devices that you'll want to make sure you have in place before he leaves:

1. Have a phone in convenient locations throughout your home. Simple and obvious step, right? It took one episode of running down the hall in the dark, tripping over a chair, and dropping the phone after I picked it up to teach me this lesson. At the beginning of David's deployment, we had three phones in our house. Now we have five.

2. If you don't already have one, get a cell phone. Keep it turned on, charged, and handy at all times.

3. Sign up for and use call forwarding. When you leave home, you can forward your phone calls to your cell phone. Why do this if you've given your loved one your cell phone number? Simple. Because you don't want to miss a call, and if he spends 10 minutes trying to get his international call through to your home, you don't want him to have to hang up and start all over again with your cell phone number. A couple of times when I was talking to David, he'd ask me for a family member's phone number, which I knew he had in his little address book. I asked about that, and he said the address book was back in his room, and his room was a 1/2-mile jog from the phones.

# Wireless Devices

One of the handiest tools I had at my fingertips was my husband's Blackberry. I was often waiting on pins and needles for an e-mail or phone call after not having heard from David in a few days. The last thing I wanted to do was go away for a weekend or even a day. That little Blackberry was great though, and it helped get me out of the house on many occasions. All we had to do was set my e-mail so that I could pick it up from wherever I was, using this wireless device. On several occasions, we went to the woods to camp for the weekend, and I would wake up on Saturday morning to see that I'd received a message from David overnight. I knew he was safe, so we could relax for the next day or two, hiking and exploring, watching wildlife or the sunset, or just reading a book or relaxing by a campfire. Being able to have that contact at all times helps to relieve some of the stress and worry that would otherwise stay in the back of your mind.

It's hard to have any kind of relaxation or happy times when you're just generally worried sick, but all these electronic devices help. It all adds up to just a bit less stress, a few extra moments of peace of mind in a very trying year.

For you, it might be a trip to Disneyland, a cruise, or an evening of bowling or just dinner and a movie, but being able to stay connected while leading as normal a life as possible is what matters most. Invest in a wireless device, and leave the house once in a while, taking your e-mail with you. You could also do this with a laptop and a wireless modem or with any of the other new electronic "toys" that come on the market every day. There are wearable computers, cell phones that you can use to access your e-mail, text messaging, and more. Use them all and stay in contact. The more contact you have, the more peace of mind you'll have.

# CHAPTER 6

# Stay Informed

From: David

Date: Wednesday, January 5, 2005, 3:48 a.m.

To: Mom

Subject: About Hillah

You will probably hear about explosions and a firefight in Hillah. It was outside of our compound, but you can tell all mothers involved that their babies are okay. Not much info at this time, it just happened, but I do have comms with everybody outside of base, and they are okay.

This was one of the most comforting messages I received during the time my son was in Iraq. The message arrived in my Inbox while I was still asleep. I got up the next morning and saw that all was well with all of David's platoon before I even read the news stories. He happened to be working in the TOC (tactical operations center) that day, so he was already at the computer when he heard the explosions outside the gate, and he was able to send this message as soon as he confirmed that everybody out patrolling was safe—and before an officer came along and shut down all outside "comms."

You have a couple of choices. You can hang on every CNN story, every evening newscast, every bit of information available, or you can take the ostrich approach and bury your head in the sand. Do whatever works for you. I know people who tell me they can't stand to watch the news; they literally put their hands over their ears and leave the room. Others want to know all they can know; they switch back and forth between Anderson Cooper and Geraldo Rivera, searching for scraps of information and a soldier they might recognize walking by in the background of every on-the-scene report.

My inclination was to face up to the facts every day. How many soldiers were killed today, and where were they? I discovered that if I knew a roadside bomb had killed three soldiers in northern Baghdad, I could mourn for those soldiers, yet I could also know that it was unlikely that my son was one of them because his patrol took him around the city of Hillah, and Hillah is about 60 miles south of Baghdad. Chances were good that he wasn't riding around on the north side of Baghdad. I mourned, but I took my comfort where I could find it.

I found that the more I knew, the better I could cope. I also found that I could not always find out all that I wanted to know just by watching TV news or reading the newspaper. I wanted more details and I wanted them fast. In this chapter I'll describe my methods for keeping current with anything newsworthy that was happening in my son's temporary neighborhood.

# No News Is . . . Just No News

In the past, the mantra of the military wife and family has been "no news is good news." In other words, if no one was knocking on your door to tell you that your loved one had been wounded or worse, you should go on about your business, confident in the knowledge that what you don't know can't hurt you. You simply knew that if something bad happened, you would find out soon enough and not have to face the truth until it was necessary. One of the things we can be very thankful for today is that news does travel fast. If your loved one is wounded or killed, most likely you will be notified within hours. But sometimes not getting an e-mail or phone call has you lying awake at night, and you just want to go searching for a sliver of comforting information right away.

Today our sons and daughters in a war zone have daily access to computers and e-mail, reporters are embedded in their units, and some of the service men and women even carry cell phones. They can contact us at any time. If they don't, there are several possible reasons, some not so appealing, and others just part of the business of war. First, they may be "busy." *Busy* is a military euphemism for fighting. Hard, mean, ugly things happen in wars, and your soldier is participating. And when he's participating, he doesn't have time to check his e-mail that day. Or something bad did happen (someone was injured or killed) and communications have been shut down until next of kin is notified. Or something bad but not so serious happened, and the officers just want the soldiers to have a chance to deal with it before they allow them to talk to relatives. This could be an ambush, a skirmish, or a battle that resulted in minor injuries and frayed nerves.

Sometimes, too, it's just not convenient for them to get to a phone or computer. There was a period of time when David's company was living at Camp Babylon (since closed because of its proximity to the ruins of the ancient city of the same name), when it was just inconvenient for him communicate often. His housing and his work area were about a mile from the nearest computer or telephone. The only way he had to get to an office where he could contact me was to walk. And the temperature was hovering near 125 degrees.

In any case, no news is no longer good news. It might be bad news, but it's probably just no news right now, and you'll hear something tomorrow. That means it's time to check the news channels, the Internet, and most importantly, to check with other families in your support group. Because of that tendency to shut down communications when something bad happens, this is when a support group formed of people whose loved ones are with your soldier is of the greatest value. If one of us in the group—Robin or Karen, Sara or Mim, Joyce or Lori, or one of many others—heard from our loved one, we spread the word. It meant that communications had not been shut down, and that meant they were all unharmed.

But remember this. More than likely, no news just means no news. My philosophy has always been there's no need to worry until I definitely know I need to worry. That philosophy was sorely tested last year, but it's still a good mindset to maintain. There are many things that can keep a soldier too busy to communicate often, and most of them are not cause for alarm.

# Beyond CNN

When you do depend on news organizations for news from the front, you quickly discover that the media in the United States chooses what and how it reports based on demographic studies, popularity, what people want to hear, and corporate sponsorship.

If the war is selling that day, if it's the "hot" story, you'll hear all about it, but if testimony in the current celebrity trial was particularly sexy, the war will be preempted in this country, or at least relegated to that crawler at the bottom of your TV screen.

It is often frustrating to try to get news of what's happening in Iraq or Afghanistan, Darfur or Korea, from the network news shows or even from CNN, Fox, or MSNBC, which all claim the news as their reason for being. They still often become preoccupied by celebrity trials, dog shows, the ups and downs of the stock market, and the latest interest hike, or resignation of a Big Ten coach. All you want to know is what kind of violence is happening where your loved one is, and you want as much detail as you can find. Often, the news you want to hear about is running across the bottom of your TV screen on that little "news crawler." And it comes in short, cryptic fragments of sentences that leave you asking more questions than it answered.

I always manage to tune in just as the end of something that sounds riveting scrolls across the screen from left to right. What was that about "...in Iraq injures dozens and kills three"? Three what? Civilians? Soldiers? What were they talking about? A bomb? A mortar attack on a U.S. base? So then, my interest piqued, I pull up a chair and wait for "the news" to be talked about, but the actual show on right now might be Larry King, who is interviewing the widow of Tony Randall, certainly not talking about Iraq or any other hot spot where U.S. military personnel are located. Nothing there for me. You can wait for that scroll to pass by again (and perhaps be interrupted this time by a commercial), you can check MSNBC where Chris Matthews is in someone's face, or click over to Fox for Bill O'Reilly's opinion on matters that do not particularly interest you. Or you can go to your computer and start looking for the real news.

The glamour has worn off the war for the major TV news outlets. They still cover it, but not to the extent you need to hear about it.

## How to Search the News Sites

All the major news outlets have Web sites, which include more of the articles that interest you and involve much more detailed reporting than you are likely to see watching the news on network or news channels. These are also available any time you want to visit them; you don't need a program schedule to access the information you want. These include:

- MSNBC
  http://www.msnbc.msn.com/
- FoxNews
  http://www.foxnews.com/
- CNN
  http://www.cnn.com/
- Reuters
  http://www.reuters.com/news.jhtml
- Associated Press
  http://www.ap.org/
- AFP, Worldwide News Agency
  http://www.afp.com/english/home/
- Yahoo!
  http://news.yahoo.com/

My preferred method of searching was to just go to the Yahoo News site and search for the keywords that pulled up stories I wanted to read. Search for the names of the town or military base where your loved one is living and working or search for the name of his outfit. If he's in the Stryker Brigade or the First Cavalry, those words are usually mentioned in stories about his unit. Or if she's in Basra or Diwaniyah, use those place names in your search.

## CAUTION

When searching, remember that different news agencies use different spellings for place names in Iraq. Here in the U.S., we tend toward the more simple spellings: Karbala, Hilla, Mosul, Kirkuk. In Europe, there may be slight differences in spelling, so if the news agency is a European one, you'll find their stories mention Kerbala and Hillah—Mosul and Kirkuk are spelled the same in all the media. Middle Eastern or Asian news agencies might even use the prefixes that are a part of the true names of some Iraqi towns: Al Kut, An Najaf, Al Hillah.

Something gets lost in the translation, but the thing you have to remember is how different place names might be spelled differently and search for all possible spellings: Karbala and Kerbala; Hilla and Hillah, Fallujah and Falluja.

My most productive news searches were often just done from the Yahoo! News page. Yahoo! isn't a news agency itself, so it gathers stories from all sources. Go to the Yahoo news page (www.yahoo.news.com) and search for the place name of the town or base of interest to you.

A search through Yahoo on March 2, 2005, for stories about *Kerbala* turned up stories from Reuters (several), Electronic Iraq, ITV.com, the New York Times, Times of Malta, and about 600 other stories from various sources.

Searching for *Karbala* resulted in 3,972 "hits" from such sources as AP, WHBF-TV in the Quad Cities, *The Des Moines Register,* CNN.com, the *Macon Telegraph,* and many more.

Obviously, the search with the more "American" spelling turned up more stories from American newspapers and news agencies. I like to get the whole story and not limit myself to the one that is somewhat tainted by commercialism or demographic studies or even American politics, so I search for both spellings. It's also just good to hear the variations in slant that agencies in Pakistan, China, or the U.K. give to the same story. Especially interesting are the Middle Eastern news outlets, such as al Jazeera.

## News from Around the World

Often, I found myself searching for news in the middle of the night. A very basic fact that you will come to be in touch with very soon is the difference in time zones between the United States and your loved one's location. If it's 3:00 in the morning here in Indiana, it's 11:00 or 12:00 in Iraq. Africa is about six hours ahead of us, Afghanistan is, oddly, eight and a half hours ahead of us, and Korea is a full 14 hours ahead of the Eastern Time Zone in the U.S. Our news distilling process doesn't start until later in the morning here, about the time the *Today Show* starts on NBC. But you want...no, you need...to hear something right now.

You will go to bed at night thinking, "It's midnight here. That means it's 8:00 a.m. in Iraq (or 8:30 in Afghanistan). She's just getting up and starting out on patrol." You say a prayer and go to bed, hoping to sleep. But if you can't, you will sometimes find yourself back up at 3:00 a.m., searching through your regular news sources, wondering if anything has happened that affected your soldier.

There are reporters and news desks elsewhere in the world who are awake right now with you.

Australian, Polish, Thai, and Indian news sources are all helpful because they are awake when you are. I found the Polish and Bulgarian reports to be especially helpful because there were Polish and Bulgarian troops in close proximity to where my son was located. Remember, we may jest about the coalition being one division of British soldiers down around Basra and a few Korean cooks, but other countries are invested in this war effort, and they often report on it. Some great places to find news before it gets to the AP wires or to MSNBC are listed here. There are many more, and if you check them out, you will find your favorites. You will no doubt find others not listed here as well.

- Bulgaria     http://www.novinite.com/
- Australia     http://www.news.com.au/
- Pakistan     http://www.jang.com.pk/thenews/
- China     http://www.xinhuanet.com/english/
- India     http://timesofindia.indiatimes.com/
- India     http://www.newsindia-times.com/
- Korea     http://southkoreanews.net/
- Thailand     http://thailandnews.net/

We have freedom of the press in the United States, but that freedom is certainly influenced and restricted by corporate ownership of the news agency or network and related political contributions, not to mention simple commercialism. Our news agencies are influenced by what sells, what's hot at the moment, and mostly, by what makes a good sound bite that they can use to pique our interest enough to entice us to "tune in at 11:00 for the full story," which turns out to be much less exciting than the earlier news flash would have you to believe. Straight news seems to

be a thing of the past here; even CNN has fallen victim to the rat-
ings wars, and the simple truth, which is all you want, is hard to
come by. Some other countries, although perhaps not quite so
democratic and not so likely to beat a drum about their freedom
of the press, still have citizens who are very interested in what's
happening in Iraq so they report on it. Sometimes they do a better job than the U.S. outlets.

## Many Views of the Same Story

Occasionally my manner of searching would turn up a story
from a Muslim country, often with an al Jazeera by-line. Sometimes I found it very interesting to hear from my son about
something that had happened, for instance the car bombing that
caused the explosion he referred to in the e-mail at the beginning
of this chapter. When he first wrote about it, he only knew there
was an explosion. Later, as the facts came to light, he learned
that it was a car bomb aimed at police recruits who were cross-
ing the road from a gymnasium to the nearby Hillah Police
Academy. That's not exactly what any of the news sources
reported, as you will see.

In this instance, I had the chance to compare what he reported
from the scene, which I knew to be true, with what was later
reported in the Western news sources, who had no one on the
scene and therefore had to rely on accounts they were given by
the U.S. military and by the Iraqi officials in Hillah. There were
reports in al Jazeera as well, this time sounding much like the
Western sources—sometimes reading a story in al Jazeera and
reading about the same event in the New York Times might make
you think you were reading about two separate occasions. So be
wary about the Middle Eastern sources. Read them, but don't
believe everything you read. You shouldn't do that anyway, no
matter where you are reading.

From a Pakistan news source,
http://www.dawn.com/2005/01/06/top9.htm

## 15 Iraqis killed in suicide bombing

HILLA, Jan 5: A suicide bomber killed 15 people at a police academy graduation on Wednesday, part of a wave of killings aimed at stopping Iraq's Jan 30 elections, but the interim prime minister vowed the vote would go ahead.

The bomber rammed an explosives-packed car into a compound in the town of Hilla, south of Baghdad, in an area known as the "Triangle of Death", and blew it up, police spokesman Hadi Hatif said.

The attack was the latest by guerrillas, who have killed more than 90 people this week alone in a campaign to sabotage the election by targeting the US-backed interim government and its fledgling security services.

From Free Speech Radio,
http://www.fsrn.org/news/20050105_news.html:

## Postpone the Iraqi Elections? (2:43)

In Iraq today, a suicide car bombing at a police station in Hilla, about 60 miles south of Baghdad, killed at least twenty people as new officers took part in a graduation ceremony. In the capital, a car bomb aimed at a US convoy killed two Iraqis and in Baquba to the northeast, a suicide car bombing at a checkpoint killed five police officers. According to the Ministry of the Interior, more than thirteen hundred police officers have been killed in the last four months. The violence has prompted a new wave of calls to postpone upcoming elections. David Enders files this report from Baghdad.

Notice that the reporter filed the story from Baghdad. He wasn't on the scene, and the focus here is on whether or not the elections should be held. A graduation ceremony was being held, but the graduation ceremony, in fact, was not the target of the car bomb, as all these stories might lead you to believe.

From an Australian news source,
http://www.theage.com.au/news/Breaking-News/Iraq:

A suicide attacker detonated his explosives-laden car outside a police academy south of Baghdad on Wednesday, killing 20 people, while another car bomb left five Iraqi policemen dead.

Iraq's prime minister said the violence would not derail landmark elections.

"We will not allow the terrorists to stop the political process in Iraq," Interim Prime Minister Ayad Allawi said, even as the death toll from the escalating insurgency reached more than 90 in the last four days.

"The elections process is the basis for the deepening of the national unity in Iraq."

The gist of the story here also concerns the upcoming election. Not many facts about the explosion other than the number of people killed, and then a nice quote from the Interim Minister about the election.

Finally, here's the story from al Jazeera. This story happens to parallel what the Western sources report, although there is much more detail.

## Iraqi police academy bombed in Hilla

Wednesday 05 January 2005, 18:06 Makka Time, 15:06 GMT

At least 22 people have been killed and others injured in a car bomb targeting a police academy in Babil district in Hilla, south of Baghdad.

Hussain al-Haidari, an Iraqi journalist, told Aljazeera a booby-trapped Daewoo car exploded on Wednesday during a graduation ceremony at the police academy.

Babil district police spokesman Hadi Hatif said the bomber drove into the compound and came under fire from police before his car exploded.

He said at least four cars and three nearby buildings were hit by the blast.

The attack came a day after a truck bomb attack on a police commando headquarters in Baghdad killed at least 11 people.

Hilla is about 100km south of the capital.

Al-Haidari said Hilla is usually calmer than other areas in Babil district such as Latifiya and Iskandariya, where clashes with US and Iraqi forces regularly take place.

Fighters have been mounting near-daily attacks on Iraqi security forces in many parts of the country ahead of the planned 30 January elections.

Notice that al Jazeera takes a more personal approach. They also refer to the insurgents as fighters and talk about "US and Iraqi forces" as if these are the "other" side and those "fighters" are on the right side. There is more personal detail, more reporting from an Iraqi point of view, and less implied criticism of the bomber. We even hear from al Jazeera what kind of car the bomber used in his attack, and they alone note that Hilla is in "the Babil district."

123

Actually, this particular report is in fairly close agreement with the Western news sources as far as reported facts are concerned. Sometimes al Jazeera and the more radical Muslim sources have an entirely different story to tell. None of these sources claims to have had a reporter on the scene, but obviously al Jazeera had someone who could tell them the make of car involved.

Again, whatever the source, try to confirm what you are reading. Don't rely on one source only for all your information.

Later that morning, I received the following e-mail from my own eyewitness after I had relayed to him what the news reports were saying:

```
From: david

To: Mom

Sent: Wednesday, January 05, 2005 9:12 AM

Subject: Re: about Hillah

It wasn't a graduation, it was the anti-terrorism
station guys training for an upcoming academy. They
are going to an academy to become eligible for
s.w.a.t., and they were all in a gymnasium across the
street from the academy exercising. When they came
out to cross the street and go to the academy, two
car bombs went off. Not official yet how many dead or
injured, but I'll let you know more when I know.
```

Later I asked David if he knew any of the Iraqi Police (or I.P.s) who were killed. The job of his platoon was to train these people to be policemen; they worked with them every day, so the question was natural—did you know any of those who were killed? His response was that he didn't think he did. He'd only notice later on if some of them didn't turn up for work. He saw the bodies, but he said they didn't look quite like themselves so it was hard to tell if he knew them or not.

Never let any of today's sterile news reporting methods convince you that war can be sanitary and conducted in a humane way. There is a certain mindset that soldiers have to attain in order to do their jobs. They have to depersonalize, even dehumanize, people who are, or may become, the enemy. They work with the Iraqis, the Afghans, and the Koreans every day, but in fact, they trust only their own buddies they trained with. Even other Coalition Forces in Iraq are not looked upon with the same sense of family as others in their own outfit. Keep this in mind when talking to your soldier. Listen more than you talk because what you think you know is based on what you learned from news sources. They simply know what they know from being on the scene, and it is often very different from what you may have heard.

Always check more than one source for any story that concerns your loved one. The examples here about the incident David alerted me to on January 5 are quite close. More often, you will find differences between the Muslim, European, and American reporting agencies. Of course, as time passes and more details are known, the stories can be honed and refined too, so a story released by Reuters, for instance, an hour after an incident won't be nearly so detailed as one released by Reuters 12 hours later.

## More Controversial Sources

You don't have to go directly to al Jazeera or al Arabya to get another slant on the news coming out of Iraq.

Also check out these alternative news sources:

- The Asheville Global Report
  http://www.agrnews.org/issues
- The Muslim News
  http://www.muslimnews.co.uk/
- Alt.muslim
  http://www.altmuslim.com/
- World Net Daily
  http://www.worldnetdaily.com/
- Islam Online
  http://www.islamonline.net/english/index.shtml

I am not endorsing or recommending any of these sources, by the way. They are there, and you should check them out with an open mind. That's all.

## NOTE

It bears repeating about the Muslim news sources: don't believe anything they say until you have confirmed it through other sources. I remember reading a report that three U.S. soldiers had been killed on the road between Najaf and Karbala. I was concerned at first because I knew David and his company traveled that road often. Throughout the day after I read that story (published by al Jazeera), I looked for confirmation or more details. Oddly, no other source repeated the story at all. It turned out that the insurgents had fired on a convoy of Marines who were passing nearby, but they didn't hit anyone, no one was hurt, no one wounded—didn't even slow the convoy down. Sometimes it seems al Jazeera reports someone's wishful thinking as news. I'm sure the insurgents who fired on that convoy wished that they had killed a few marines, but it just wasn't true.

# My Ways to Gather News

The Internet, in particular, abounds in news sources. You can get your news from TV and radio, from the evening network news, or from those TV channels that purport to be all about news, but may, in fact, be more about entertainment. I found them to be lacking, and I preferred finding out what I wanted to know about the situation in Iraq, especially as it affected my son, in my own way.

I did two things to ensure that I never missed a story that might involve David and his company. First of all, I set up my Yahoo! home page to display all news stories coming from the Middle East.

If you don't already have My Yahoo! set up, go to Yahoo! and set up your own Yahoo page:

1. Type www.yahoo.com in the address bar of your browser and press Enter.

2. Click on My Yahoo! and follow the instructions to set up your personal Yahoo page.

3. At the top of the My Yahoo page, next to the words New User, click on Sign Up.

4. The Registration page appears. Complete the information requested there, and your Yahoo page will appear.

After you have set up your personal Yahoo page, follow these steps to have Yahoo search for and display all the news stories you want to read:

1. Click the Add Content button at the top of the page.

2. In the Find Content box, enter the words of the area you'd like to target: Middle East, Iraq, Afghanistan, Korea, Asia, Africa, or any area of the world you're interested in.

3. A list of sources appears. Click the Add button next to as many news sources as you'd like to include on your page.

You can then arrange your page so that the stories you want to read first will appear as soon as you log on to Yahoo.

I also signed up for e-mail alerts from Google every time the words Hilla or Karbala appeared in a news story. I could have included the alternate spelling of Kerbala, but using the American spelling limited what turned up in my Inbox to only those stories that made it to the American press. I still went to my search page and searched for Kerbala, but the e-mails always appeared if anything of interest to me happened. Usually someone somewhere reported something about one of those cities, so every day when I checked my e-mail, there were at least a couple of Google alerts. The morning of January, 5, the day much of this chapter has focused on, there were more than 10 alerts. A few other stories turned up about an artist named, I believe, Hilla Becher, but it was easy to sort those out from the ones I wanted to read.

1. From the Google taskbar at the top of your browser window, search for the town, military unit, or area of the world of interest to you.

2. On the right side of the screen, usually beneath several pictures associated with your search, you'll see a little bell icon with the words "Alert me when news items match [your search term].

3. Click on the bell icon and Google will deliver all the stories it finds that match your search term to your Inbox.

## Silly Questions by Newscasters or How to Make a Military Mom Really Mad

Remember the story from November 9, 2004 of the young marine who was featured in a *Los Angeles Times* photo after he had just spent days in a major battle for Fallujah? He appeared with greasepaint on his face, what can only be described as war-weary eyes, and a cigarette dangling from his lip. His father is quoted as saying "'Boy, this person looks like he's 30.'"

That young man, James Blake Miller, of Kentucky, was referred to in the media as "the face of war" and "the Marlboro man."

See http://www.omaha.com/index.php?u_np=0&u_pg=54&u_sid=1346947 for a full story on Miller's return home and his life after all the media attention.

One of the newscasters from MSNBC or CNN contacted his mother and interviewed her live on TV. She asked, "Did your son smoke before he went to Iraq?" When the mother answered no, her next question was "What did you think? Did it upset you to see him smoking?"

I was up and out of my seat that day because I wanted to give the answer. Miller's mother was polite. I don't think I could have been. I really don't remember what her response was, but I know what mine would have been: "I would have been happy to see him smoking crack at that particular juncture." How dare that reporter focus on the inane act of smoking? He still had a head and he still was able to smoke, and I know that's all his mother could see. He was alive! And that is all that mattered. War kills you here and now; smoking takes a while, and you can quit later after you get home.

See the sidebar for some things some learned people have had to say regarding soldiers and smoking. I think some reporters need to read this before they ask any more useless and inane questions of mothers back home. The next one they interview might not be so polite.

I have more to say on the subject of tobacco use among soldiers in Chapter 2, "Supplies." Let me just say now that, in this mother's opinion, while he's in a war zone is not the time to nag your loved one about his bad habits. That's another campaign for another day.

# Soldiers, Smoking, and the Media

Why do soldiers smoke? Why do baseball players chew tobacco?

Karl Ginzel, a pharmacologist at the University of Arkansas performed experiments with cats in which he injected nicotine into the right atrium of their hearts, which contains blood that is bound for their lungs.

Two things happened to those cats: they became more alert, and their muscles relaxed—at the same time.

Most drugs are used for pleasure. Tobacco has been called the workplace drug. It can be compared to both Valium and caffeine, taken by workers to keep their skills sharp or, more precisely, to keep their skills from deteriorating on the job because of such things as lack of sleep, an overwrought nervous system, or the . . . working day.

Valium and caffeine can be taken to get "high," but they are most often taken to get "normal."

In an experiment, Norman Heimstra at the University of South Dakota, had subjects watch a film on the bombing of Hiroshima and Nagasaki: nonsmokers had much greater fluctuations in their mood states than did smokers who smoked over the course of . . . the experience.

Under a stressful set of experiments on monkeys (which I will not detail here) nicotine decreased their attack behavior, but it increased the escape response. The drugs it was similar to in this regard were not opiates or amphetamines, but tranquilizers. It showed the same pattern as chlordiazepoxide, which is better known by its trade name, Librium.

"Smokers use nicotine's control to moderate their attentional states. That is, they're not using nicotine to exaggerate their state in one direction or another, but to normalize it; to arouse themselves from boredom or calm themselves from overstimulation...People may want to get high on amphetamines, they may want to get low on Quaaludes, but they seem to want to get medium on nicotine. They often seem to be seeking a normality that their environment has taken them out of."

From http://www.wramc.amedd.army.mil/education/
tobaccohistory.htm

Use of tobacco among World War II soldiers had an extraordinary effect on relieving the tedium of war, but hooked an entire generation into nicotine addiction. Lucky Strikes were free and tobacco companies made it a patriotic duty to contribute to the war effort. Such was the importance of tobacco use among troops that when asked General John J. Pershing said, "You ask me what we need to win the war? I answer tobacco as much as bullets."

Footnote text: Information quoted from Smoking, the Artificial Passion by David Krogh, W.H. Freeman and Co. (Sd) 1991.

Newscasters also don't always seem to be certain where anything is in the Middle East. I have heard them say that Hilla is in the southern part of Baghdad (it is about 60 miles south of the city) or that Fallujah is in the western part of Baghdad (it is west of the city). It seems as if some of the reporters confuse Baghdad with all of Iraq. That may be understandable because there aren't very many reporters throughout the country any more; the ones that are there are almost always "reporting live from Baghdad."

It's understandable, but it's unforgivable. If I can figure out where these towns and cities and military camps are and can tell the difference between Marine Corps digital cammo desert BDUs and the regular desert BDUs of the Army, I expect the people who report the news to do their research and be able to do the same thing. If I can figure out the geography of a country on the other side of the world that had never interested me before, if I can figure out how to pronounce Mosul and Kabul and Darfur, surely the people who are paid to pronounce it ought to be able to do it correctly. After all, I'm an ordinary civilian. I had no experience with the military at all until three years ago when my 31-year-old son announced his decision to join so he could go and fight the terrorists who had attacked his country.

# Conclusion

You may not be the type of person who "needs to know" as I am. If so, you won't want to search the Internet for news stories every day as I learned to do. I think you should do the thing that helps you cope best with this experience that has been thrust upon you. I simply like being in control and that control helped me to stay sane during an insane time. After the December 22, 2004, bombing of a dining tent in Mosul, several friends and family members called me, asking quietly if I'd heard from David that day. When I asked if they were especially concerned for any reason, it turned out that they had heard about the high number of casualties and wanted to know if he was all right. Mosul is about 200 miles north of Baghdad; Hilla, where I knew David to be, is about 60 miles south of the capitol. Paying attention to geography, time-lines, and information gleaned from dozens of sources told me that it was highly unlikely that my son was in that tent that day. Better, I think, to be as informed as possible, and the best way to be informed is to gather information from as many sources as possible.

In Part III I discuss organizations and individuals you'll want to reach out to. The families of others in your loved one's unit, support personnel in the military, your priest or rabbi, friends and family—during this year of high tension and stress, you are going to need some support and help, some prayers, and some words of assurance. Set up your support network early, stay in touch, and don't hesitate to reach out and ask for help when you need it.

# PART III

# Support from Organizations and Individuals

You may find yourself, during the time of your child's deployment, in need of some sort of "official" support. You may already have been given some contact information. You may also find yourself in need of some "unofficial" support. Sometimes you just need a shoulder to cry on or someone to talk to when you're awake in the middle of the night, hanging on the latest version of a news story that broke during the 11:00 p.m. news on CNN. You're waiting for further details and biting your nails, but the rest of your circle of family and friend support are all sleeping.

In Chapter 7, I'll tell you about some of the situations encountered by my family and others I became familiar with when a family member at home just needed a little extra help. I'll tell you what the military will and will not do for you and what other organizations you might need to turn to when you've reached the limits of military help. I'll tell you which

135

organizations you should contact in which circumstances, which organizations might be contacting you, and I'll give you my assessment of those groups. Some are dependable and trustworthy; others might be. Sometimes it just seems to depend on the individuals involved.

In Chapter 8, I'll tell you the story of our little group. A group of about 75 people I stayed in contact with, some of whom have become lifelong friends. We accomplished a great deal while sharing with and caring for each other, and I think we did a great job of supporting the soldiers of the 66th MP Company during their deployment. They would have been fine without us, but I know we made a difference, and that was important to the soldiers and to us as well.

You may think that all of the concern and worry and caring are one way—going from you to your son or daughter. The fact is, they worry more about what we hear and know than we are aware. They are there to protect democracy and freedom and the American way of life, and get this: we represent that way of life to them. They see themselves as protecting that way of life through us by protecting us from some of the more frightful things they see and do. It was important to all of them to know that their families were supporting each other and bonding back home while they risked their lives for something they believed in.

# CHAPTER 7

# Official Help

Friday, January 23, 2004, 3:01 a.m.

From: David

To: Mom

Subject: (none)

Mom, the following information is who you can get hold of to get information about what is going on while I am in Iraq. You can e-mail him whenever you want, and you can request that he e-mail you with any information and newsletters about our company and what we are doing. He can only give you certain information, I'm sure, but he is the best way for you to find out whatever he can tell you. His name is SFC Sparks,* and he's a pretty nice guy. His e-mail address is [blacked out] and [blacked out]; his home phone is xxx-xxx-xxxx and his cell phone is xxx-xxx-xxxx. If you just want information, I would say to just e-mail him, but if there is a problem in the family, or you receive some mail or any information about me that could turn into, or already is, a serious problem, then you can call him and let him know about it. Then he will contact the company and they will help me to solve it.

My only thing about that is, if it is something that
I can fix without the company knowing about it, then
that's the best way. If it's something that I
absolutely cannot fix from Iraq, then go ahead and
call him, just think about what the problem is, and
if it might cause me some grief (shit) from the
commander or the First Sgt., and it could be fixed
with a phone call from you about my current situation
(being in Iraq, fighting for my country), than that
would be the best. SFC Sparks is the NCOIC of the
rear detachment, and will help with anything and will
keep you informed by e-mail if you ask him to. I'll
talk to you tomorrow.

*Sparks is an alias. Names have been changed to avoid embarrassment for individuals no longer associated with the Army.

Every branch of the service provides support for family members during times of need. You may need to get an emergency message to a loved one, you may need assistance with care of a dependent, you may have burning questions that only someone in authority can answer or that only a phone call from your loved one can solve.

Following are some of the support personnel I came in contact with while my son was in Iraq, and a couple I'm very happy I never had to meet in their official capacity. But they're there when you need them, and that's a comfort in itself.

# Rear Detachment Commander

This is the first person I want to talk about because he is your most immediate help in time of crisis or just to help you understand the intricacies or protocol in your particular branch of the service. The families of the 66th were blessed with the soft spoken, insightful, intelligent, and wise SFC D. Sparks. We couldn't have asked for a better liaison to interpret for us what was and was not being said in the communiqués we received. He was there with us and for us every day of that year, and he stayed calm in the face of storm. He told us what he could, and he was very patient when we kept insisting that he tell us things he could not tell us. When I think of the Rudyard Kipling poem "If," I think of SFC Sparks. He kept his head when all about him were losing theirs.

I first heard about SFC Sparks when I received the e-mail that begins this chapter a few weeks before David and his unit left the country. SFC Sparks stayed in contact through the whole year. There wasn't much he could tell us, but he told us what he could. His messages were usually cryptic, but they left me knowing that all was as well as it could be under the circumstances. Of course, I contacted SFC Sparks right away; I wrote him a well-thought-out graceful note, introducing myself and telling him David had suggested I contact him. His reply:

```
Maam,

All is taken care of - You are added to the list.
```

I received the following message from Sparks when the unit arrived in Kuwait:

```
Greetings,

The plane did arrive safely in Kuwait. When I get
more information that I can release, like an actual
mailing address, I will send it out.
```

As I said, SFC Sparks was cryptic, a man of few words, but he was informative. As the year wore on, he got to know some of us a bit better, and his messages became a bit more relaxed, but still there wasn't much he could tell us except to say all was well and morale was high. That was about all we really needed to know anyway.

He was the rear detachment commander (NCOIC, or non-commissioned officer in command), which means that he was in charge of the platoon that was left at Ft. Lewis while the rest of the company deployed. That platoon that remained behind had their hands full with paperwork and support to do here for the rest of the company. They still needed to have payroll processed and personnel and equipment matters handled, and that's what the rear detachment does. As rear detachment commander, he was also in charge of dealing with the families and trying to steer them towards the proper channels when they needed help.

## What the Rear Detachment Commander Does and Does Not Do

The rear detachment commander can help you with any military problems you have. If you're a wife and you're having trouble with a change of address or getting some insurance matter settled, call the rear detachment officer. He can't really solve your problem himself, but he can tell you who to call, what forms to fill out, or what to say. The military is probably the most bureaucratic employer any of us will ever have to deal with. There are forms for everything, and if you don't have the right form, you are lost.

I watched as SFC Sparks helped wives and family members handle everything from movers who didn't show up to babies who arrived ahead of schedule. He was the coordinator for the Family Readiness Group (FRG) and sent out regular announcements of their meetings. As a matter of fact, I think in our case, SFC Sparks and his soldiers handled a lot of things that were usually supposed to be handled by the FRG.

For instance, we all got monthly phone calls from the soldiers at Ft. Lewis. Just a polite call and a private on the line who said, "Good morning, ma'am. This is PFC Jenkins with the 66th MP Company at Ft. Lewis. I'm calling to tell you that all is well with your soldier in Iraq, and to ask how you are getting along."

Sometimes I tried to pump that caller for more information, but it didn't really get me anywhere. My response was usually "We're fine here." And that was the end of the conversation. It seemed useless, but it was also comforting.

Why did they do that? Well, people do tend to move from time to time or they do have problems that need addressing. Sometimes there would be an extra question or two. Once it was "we're checking to see how long it's been since you heard from your soldier." My first thought was, "Jeez, did you lose him?" But the truth, I later guessed, was that some of them had grown lax about communication with home, and some families had complained about it. By the way, the worst thing a mother can do is call and say, "I haven't heard from my son in two weeks. Why aren't you letting him write?"

Well, one thing the military encourages is writing to your mother. Before David's company left Kuwait to head in-country, I got a note from him. I had gotten a phone call the same day that letter was written, but it didn't matter to his commanders. They told every one of them to sit down, write a letter, put it in an envelope, and mail it home before they left. He was under orders to write me a letter. As far as the Army was concerned, that was one potential problem dealt with.

# Family Readiness Group (FRG)

Okay, now it gets a little dicey. I never did quite understand what the FRG was able to do for me. As far as I could tell, they were a social group on post, a group of wives who lived at the fort while their husbands were away. They shopped together, had coffee together, babysat each other's kids, and were just friends. I don't know this, but I believe their social status within the group depended on their husband's rank. They kept insisting that I was a member, but if I was, that membership seemed to be without much substance.

We had difficulties with our particular group. They kept saying, "You're all members of the FRG," but when we said, "Okay, what does the FRG do?" they had no answer. I occasionally received messages from SFC Sparks announcing a chili supper or a lingerie party, but first of all I was in Indiana and they were in Washington, and second of all, I didn't really need them as a social support system. I had a life here.

I know from others in the military that the FRG can operate differently, so I think the quality of support you get from this organization depends on the individuals who are at each unit's helm. I expect ours did a good job there on post for the wives and families who lived there. Mothers and other family members, however, have different needs. We don't need a ride to work or help with a flat tire or a babysitter. What we do need sometimes is a little psychological and emotional support, and the military just doesn't really have a very efficient setup for taking care of us.

I believe one of the services this group should provide is something called a phone tree. Whenever there is news that needs to be passed quickly through the ranks of the families, the phone tree is put in motion. The commander's or the first sergeant's spouse back home calls all the platoon sergeant's spouses. Each of them, in turn, calls the designated point of contact for each person in her husband's platoon. Each of them then calls the squad leaders' spouses. And each of them calls the people in her husband's squad. (Insert the word mother, sister, aunt, father, uncle, or brother where appropriate, but this is usually done by wives and mothers.) In this way, information can be passed to a lot of people quickly.

Generally, the phone tree in the FRG might more or less follow the chain of command in the company. It might, but it doesn't have to. The leader of the FRG is usually the wife who has the most seniority as an Army wife. I don't think this is any hard and fast rule; it's just the way it usually works out.

Things have changed a bit in this age of technology, and most of us have computers and e-mail, so information can be passed even more quickly from one person to many with one mouse click. But I never did get an e-mail or a phone call from anyone in the FRG. I believe that is why we got our calls from the soldiers back at the fort. The Army needed to keep track of anyone who moved or whose phone number had changed anyway, so it worked out well.

I've also figured out that one reason I was not ever contacted by the FRG might be that I was not listed as David's primary point of contact. He had listed his father as the person to contact in case of his death, so that may have made me an outsider as far as the FRG is concerned. Of course, I don't believe they ever contacted his father either, so I just don't really know. You might want to investigate and find out just how the FRG works in your soldier's unit.

You'll learn a lot more about this in the next chapter. Our group of mothers, wives, and aunts, spread from North Carolina to Florida to Michigan to Washington and Texas, was able to establish our own support network. It worked for us. We got the support and love there, the "sit up all night and worry with me" kind of support that was lacking from the military support group set up to serve that purpose for us.

I consider myself a nonmilitary person with a loved one in the military. I'm not a part of that lifestyle, but I am out here on the fringes, looking in and trying to learn what I need to know to support my son.

# Chaplain

You've all heard it said that there are no atheists in foxholes. It's certainly true that one of the things you will undergo during your soldier's deployment is spiritual growth. People who aren't particularly religious, who don't pray regularly before meals or at bedtime, who don't attend church, suddenly find themselves driving down the street or vacuuming the carpet or steering a cart through the aisles of Costco, feeling as if they could burst into tears from the fear of it all, but mostly from the general feeling that something might be happening that is beyond your control.

You just find yourself with nowhere to turn but to God. We said things in my family that we had never before so urgently felt the need to put into words: "God be with you." "God protect you." "I love you." Almost overnight it became important to actually speak these words. We thought them often in the past, but now we were saying them.

Every package I sent to David included a packing list. And every packing list included what I came to call "warrior angels." I consciously prayed as I packed each box and asked angels to go with it and protect my son and his buddies.

## How They Help Soldiers

Chaplains are posted with all units deployed anywhere. There's always a chaplain available and belief in a higher power is a large part of military service, although atheists and agnostics are supported as well. Chaplains in real life may be priests, rabbis, imans, and ministers. They may be of any religious branch, but they all can perform the rites of other religious groups.

Technically, a chaplain who in real life is a Baptist minister is able to give Catholic communion. They all have special expanded rights and duties that allow this. It's called "serving all faiths," and I think we could all take a lesson from these men and women who reach across the barriers and boundaries of sect and belief to provide strength and minister to the souls of men and women who are in harm's way every day. They are the morale officers, the ones who try to keep a finger on the pulse of the soldiers' mental and emotional wellbeing.

The duties of chaplains are:

- Provide religious services for all. They perform the rites and ceremonies of all religions.

- Provide pastoral care for all. This means they are there if a soldier needs to be informed of a death in his family back home, or if he is in need of comfort because of a personal crisis or just needs someone to understand and listen.

- They also take part in the character, moral, and ethical growth of the soldiers under their care. They provide services to improve morale and they provide non-threatening, uncritical resources for the soldiers when they need it.

Chaplains do not carry weapons.

## The Chaplain and You

What does all this have to do with you? I believe that if I thought my son or another military member I cared about was depressed to the point of suicide or just troubled and in need of emotional guidance and concern, I might contact the chaplain of his unit myself. I don't know of anyone who did because, amazingly, the soldiers of the 66th stayed in remarkably good mental health, and their morale remained high. But if I was certain that I discerned a problem, I would most certainly speak up about it, and the chaplain would probably be the person I would contact.

# Some Circumstances When the Military Will Contact You

Most of the time, the military prefers not to have to deal with families any more than they have to. One of the little military clichés I heard was, "Never piss off a soldier's mom." They did tread lightly with us, called us ma'am, were just overly polite and respectful. I don't know. Maybe it was mostly genuine; on the other hand, there was always a sense I had of being "handled."

Under some circumstances though, you'll get genuine help and care from the branch of military your child is attached to. When things get rough, you do get personal, caring treatment.

## Casualty Notification

Okay, so if the worst happens, how will you find out? Or what if your son or daughter is wounded in action, taken gravely ill, or injured or even killed in a non-combat incident—how will you find out?

There is a protocol for notification. First of all, if it is at all possible, your son or daughter will be encouraged to call you. I've heard stories of wounded soldiers being handed a cell phone as they were being prepped for surgery so their next of kin could have the assurance of hearing a familiar voice saying, "Mom, I'm going to be okay." That is preference number one. Let the soldier tell his family back home about his injuries himself.

But, again, what if the worst happens? The following is an excerpt from Army Regulation 600-8-1:

> In the event of death or missing status, the individual's primary next of kin (PNOK) and secondary next of kin (SNOK) will be notified in person by a uniformed service representative, and a casualty assistance officer will be designated for the PNOK.

We need to go back a step now to define PNOK and SNOK. Early in his military career, your soldier was asked to list the one person he wanted notified in case of his death. He is the one who chooses whose door gets the knock. If he's married, this will invariably be his wife. If not, it will be a parent. In the case of divorced parents, he has to choose one as his PNOK. He will be asked to update that designation just before he deploys.

What that paragraph from Army Regulations means is that two people will come, in person, to knock on your door if your soldier is declared to be missing or dead. It doesn't matter whether he's killed in combat or dies in a vehicle accident. Someone will knock on your door.

The only exception to this is if it seems likely that you may find out about his death through other means, such as a newscast or other media report from the front. In that case, the Army, in order to get word to you quickly, might handle notification with a phone call. They would then follow that up as quickly as possible with a personal visit, and they would continue to stay in contact until you had gotten all the help and advice, including applying for survivor benefits and other personnel-related claims, that would be your due.

Any other injury or wound will usually be reported to you by telephone.

# Some Observations on the Casualties of War

There can be no such thing as an objective look at the loss of even one young, healthy American in war. I think war is passè. We should have better ways of solving our differences. But, there our children are—fighting in a foreign land—dying in a foreign land. So, here, just to help you get your head around the reality, is as close as I can come to being objective about this topic. I believe if you face your demons, you render them impotent. This was a very hard one to face, but here's what I discovered.

First, we need to define a few terms. The term *casualty* includes all of the following:

- KIA: killed in action
- MIA: missing in action
- POW: prisoner of war
- WIA: wounded in action
- WIA-RTA: wounded in action/returned to duty within 72 hours

## NOTE

By the way, OIF is Operation Iraqi Freedom. OEF is Operation Enduring Freedom, and it refers to the current mission/operation in Afghanistan.

You can find casualty statistics and trends at the following Web page.

http://icasualties.org/oif/

The Department of Defense provides these numbers at the following page:

http://www.defenselink.mil/news/

You must click on the link titled OIF/OEF Casualty Update, which will take you to an Adobe Acrobat file that contains the information you seek.

Explore these pages. What you learn may either alarm or somehow comfort you. Of course, the statistics change every day, but you can get a good feel here for spikes in enemy action, trends, number of troops injured in each province, number of troops injured from the various countries participating in Operation Iraqi Freedom, and more.

The numbers change every day, but at the moment the number of troops killed in action in relation to the number of troops killed in non-combat accidents is about 4 to 1. That is, about one fifth of the total reported military casualties in Iraq are the result of an accident. Actually, it's 78% from hostile fire and 22% accidental. None of this really matters when it's your loved one who is killed, of course. I just want you to be able to keep those numbers in perspective.

Here's another interesting statistic you'll find on those casualty Web pages: Over 15,000 soldiers have been wounded in action. As of this writing, November 15, 2005, the total number of wounded is 15,568. More than half of those (8,357) were returned to duty within 72 hours. This seems to be a result of better body armor and better protection all round.

Many more have been wounded in action than have been killed in action. It appears the technology of warfare is actually resulting in fewer lives lost. Just as many shots are fired, and this war in Iraq has introduced the concept of improvised explosive devices (IEDs) and vehicle-borne improvised explosive devices (V-BIDs), better known to us as roadside bombs and car bombs, but our soldiers are surviving being fired upon more often.

Hundreds of thousands have served in Iraq and Afghanistan. If they had all stayed home, the fact is some of them would have died here in accidents and from criminal activity. I mention this to help you keep your worry in perspective. Of course you are more scared than you would be if he were in college and had gone out to a party with his friends. But he could be killed driving home from a party too. Iraq and Afghanistan are dangerous places, and no one wants their loved one to be there. People are shooting at them all the time, and they are in daily danger. Just trust God, their excellent training, their body armor, and armored vehicles to keep them safe. It's really all you can do.

Most have body armor; if yours isn't in an armored vehicle, see elsewhere in this chapter for some suggestions on where to start campaigning.

# But Who Do You Call When You Need Help

In what situations do you need help? Who can you call for that help? How you ask for help and who you ask for help should be determined by the seriousness of your situation.

As David's e-mail at the beginning of this chapter indicates, try to solve the problem yourself. If you can't take care of it without his involvement, try to wait until you can talk to him. If the problem won't wait, contact the rear detachment commander, explain the situation, and ask that your soldier be contacted and asked to call you immediately.

I can't possibly list all the things that might happen to you or to your soldier's business affairs, marriage, or other family emergencies. You just have to make these judgments for yourself and weigh the importance and the critical nature of the problem. If it is important but can wait, it should wait. If it's not so important but has to be done today, make the decision yourself and leave the soldier alone. If it's of critical importance and needs immediate attention, then you should probably try to reach him.

Here's a list of people and organizations that I contacted myself or situations I know of in which someone contacted an outside agency during the year our soldiers were in Iraq and the reasons we contacted them:

**Politicians:** I wrote a letter to the two senators from Indiana and a couple of others who seemed to be most directly involved with the military when I thought David's company was in danger because of being under the command of another country's army. It's a fine line between working with someone and working for someone, and that line was crossed a few times, and I thought it was not legal, so I complained. I complained politely and I spoke in general terms, describing the situation, but not giving any details, because I knew my son's life was in danger. However, I also knew that I could cause problems for him if my action became known. It seemed worth it at the time though, and I would do it again.

Did it help? Probably not, but Senator Lugar's office thought my plea was valid enough to forward it to the Department of the Army. Several months later, I got a reply telling me that sometimes the changing situation on the battlefield made chain of command a bit unclear. It was not a satisfying answer, but I simply felt better because I knew I did all I could to help change the situation.

**Red Cross:** When nothing else will do and you need that military person in your family to come home right away—there's a death in the family or some other dire circumstance—contact the Red Cross.

While David was at home for his two-week leave during deployment, we had a death in our family. He still had to contact the Red Cross and get a two-day extension to his leave so that he could be here for the funeral, but arrangements were made through them with his commanders, we received a condolence letter from the captain and the first sergeant, and he simply got on a plane on Monday instead of Saturday. You must follow proper procedure and protocol in the event of a death in the family, and that means call the Red Cross.

**News Media:** If things are looking really bad and you think your soldier is in danger due to bad decisions made by his commanders, call the press. That is your right as an American citizen. If you yell loud enough and have a good enough reason, you might see your loved one's name and face on television.

Remember the transportation unit that was asked to go into hostile territory with unsafe equipment? Remember the daughter who left a message on her mother's answering machine saying, "Please, Mom, get the word out"?

The troops of the Army Reserve 343rd Quartermaster Company, 19 in number, refused to take seven trucks that they deemed to be unsafe (unarmored and unable to go more than 40 miles per hour) on a road to Baghdad where military convoys came under daily attack from insurgents. They were read their rights and placed under arrest, possibly facing dishonorable discharge or perhaps even more serious punishment.

That situation resulted in a congressional investigation and full media exposure. When the families heard about the situation, they called the press. At least the families of those soldiers knew their loved ones would be treated fairly because the Army was under the scrutiny of the press. Yell loud if you have to. If you know the circumstances warrant your taking action, you will not regret speaking out.

You are a civilian, and your loved one is in the military. He is there fighting for your right to speak and be heard in a democracy. So please don't hesitate to speak out. Yes, you must keep Op Sec (Operation Security) in mind at all times, but don't worry. Your soldier isn't going to tell you anything that is to be kept secret anyway. He's much too professional to do that.

# Wrapping Up

There's help available if you know where to look. Talk to people. Ask other family members. Talk to the rear detachment commander, the FRG, and anyone else you know who might be able to give advice about your particular situation. Most of all, talk to all the new friends you've made who have loved ones serving with your soldier.

I looked at it this way. If my son had been killed because of that flaw in the chain of command that I thought existed with another country's military and if I had not complained to someone, I'd have to live with that knowledge the rest of my life. I put my complaint in writing and sent it to someone who could make a difference. I was not about to let anything unnecessary happen because of an arrangement that I knew about and that I could make some noise about.

I exercised my right as a citizen of a free country to speak out. I would do it again, and you should too if you see something that needs to be corrected.

# CHAPTER 8

# Emotional Support

To: Karen

From: Sandy

Date: Wednesday, December 15, 2004, 7:13 p.m.

Subject: RE: bomb

Well, I haven't heard from David since last night. He warned me that they'd be moving today, but said he'd still be working in the TOC tonight. But he wasn't quite sure that there would be a computer or phone at Camp Charlie. Just have to wait and hold my breath, I guess. I also have this fear that if I don't hear from him it's because there is a communications lockdown because some incident has occurred.

I think the Sunnis are gonna be active in their area now, and I think they're gonna go after the Shi'ite politicians. Because, in a fair election, the Shi'ites outnumber the Sunnis 6 to 4, and they'll put their boys in office. Saddam was a Sunni, and the Sunnis are used to being rich and powerful.

They set off a car bomb on the road between Karbala and Hilla last week. And then the big bomb today in Karbala. And really, you know, Karbala, Babylon,

Hilla, and Kut--they're all just a stone's throw away from each other. They are all in the Tigris/Euphrates River Valley, fertile, green, unlike the rest of the country, which is mostly desert. Najaf is a bit further south, but not a long way, and it's in the desert.

----- Original Message -----

From: Karen

To: Sandy

Sent: Wednesday, December 15, 2004 12:15 PM

Subject: bomb

Sandy,

Robin just sent me an ABC online news bulletin. It was a convoy of Iraqis that were at Salman Pak near a nuclear plant that was attacked. I just remember in last month's newsletter it said 1st platoon was assisting with protection of Iraqi trainees after the awful execution of that busload.

Yep, something is weird today. Don't know what but it is. We never hear about the injured even if they get their arms or legs blown off.

Keep in touch if you see anything else.

Karen

You are about to go to a place you've never been before. Well, you've probably been there for short periods of time. But this time you'll be there for several months.

If you're like most parents, you've been through all the scary things that parents go through. You stayed awake all night when your baby was cranky with a cold. You watched as she went out the door on the first day of school. You watched over her when she had her tonsils out. You sat up waiting when she was late getting home from a night out with friends. As the parent of a soldier, you have waited for her to have a chance to call you from basic training. You've worried for short periods of time, a day, a night, a week or two, and you've worried when you knew there was danger. But you've never watched her get on a plane to go to a war zone, and you've never worried like you are about to be worried—and this time the anxiety will last for several months.

# Your Usual Circle of Friends and Supporters May Not Be Enough

Maybe you have a tight circle of friends and family who stick together through everything. There are all sorts of situations and family arrangements and all sorts of loyalty within them. What most of us found was that our friends and family, no matter how loyal, loving, and caring under most circumstances, could only go so far with us in our fearful year. Some of them sent CARE packages, some hung banners in their windows and ribbons on their porches. Some stuck those magnetic Support Our Troops ribbons on their cars.

They asked often if we'd heard anything lately from our soldier. They showed all the care and concern that they were able to show. And yet, sometimes they just didn't "get" us. They cared and were concerned, but they were not glued to the news channels and the Internet news pages as we were. It was possible for them to spend more than five minutes without having their thoughts turn to the Middle East.

Your friends are always there for you. They'll diet with you, exercise with you, and tape "Desperate Housewives" for you. They are about to notice a difference in you though. They'll be worried and concerned for a while with you, and then most of them will be worried and concerned about you. They'll have to return to their normal pursuits, and you aren't able to do that just yet. When they meet you for lunch, you will have some new worry lines. You'll be distracted. They'll worry about you, but they won't know how to help.

All the people in your life have responsibilities of their own. They have jobs, families, school, and hobbies. You seem to be focused on only one thing, and most of them won't be able to share that laser-like focus with you. They care, but they aren't obsessed, and you . . . well, you are.

They can't all go where you are in this year-long crisis in your life. In fact, what they begin to do is worry about you, tell you that you need to "snap out of it" and get on with your own life. There may be something in that advice, but what I found was that it made me mad.

Of course, you have other concerns in your life too, other children, other people you care about, a job...but all those things will be taking a backseat to that one scary thought that never goes away: did my child live through this day?

## Physician/Counselors

After a few months of waking up in the middle of the night to check e-mail, staying wide awake for a couple of hours, and then prayerfully crawling back in bed, only to feel groggy and sleep-deprived the next day, I decided to ask my doctor if he would be willing to give me something to help me sleep. Well, no, he wasn't, and he didn't think drugs were the answer for my problem. He said I needed someone to talk to and if I couldn't find friends or family to do that with, he'd send me to a therapist. All I needed was a friend, a really good friend, one who could share my pain and fear.

I said I'd see what I could do, but I knew I'd already tried to make this connection with my large circle of "regular" friends, and to no avail. Nobody in my "regular" life really quite understood what I was going through.

Then I remembered an e-mail I had gotten from SFC Sparks a few months before:

```
groups.msn.com/66th MP Company/support*

This was put together by a Family Member and she has
done a great job.

Just take a look and see if it is something that
will work for you.
```

*This site has been taken down now, so the link is no longer active.

159

# About Stress

As a middle-aged American with health care provided by an HMO, I hear a lot about stress and how to avoid it. It's one of those heart health risk factors that I'm told could make my blood pressure go through the roof, make me gain weight around my middle, and help me on my way to a heart attack.

I'm encouraged to try deep breathing, to listen to soothing music, to learn to let go. That advice might work for the kind of stress you encounter on your morning commute or in dealing with your daughter's new boyfriend. I've tried it before. It's nice to close your eyes and chill out to the music of a flute.

When it comes to the absolute, life and death, fight or flight, stress of knowing your child is being shot at on a daily basis though, these stress reduction tricks are a lot like spitting in the wind. No amount of mind control, massage, acupuncture, or any other relaxation therapy is going to fix that.

By all means, you should get a massage, practice deep breathing, and whatever else offers a bit of solace to your troubled heart and body. Even a hot bath helps. Just don't expect miracles from it in this situation. As a matter of fact, telling me I needed to relax and eat more fruit was a sure way to make my blood pressure rise.

I call what we were going through "situational stress," and the only cure for that is to change the situation. Relaxation therapy and other stress reducers are only stopgaps when you have ongoing, real world stress that is inescapable.

# Peer Support Group

At this time, David had been in Iraq for about five months. I had been to the Web site before, had posted and introduced myself, had read a few posts by other mothers, wives, fathers, aunts, and uncles. But I had never really reached out to anyone there, never tried to make a real connection with another human being.

So the day the doctor told me to "find someone to talk to about this," I went there looking to really connect with someone, someone who was in my shoes, someone who was feeling the same things I was feeling, the same fear, the same obsession for knowing. I was looking to relieve some of my anxiety by sharing it with someone else.

I figured I'd try this, and if I was still beside myself with worry and fear, I'd go back and demand a pill for it, or at least a therapist to talk to about the troubled times I was going through.

## Find a Support Group

I was lucky. Someone had actually had the foresight to set up a Web site, to reach out to other family members of the 66th. She had asked for and received a list of e-mails, she had gone to MSN and set up the site, she had sent out invitations. She had checked into and made the effort to reach out to all the other family members of the 66th.

She set up the Web site, she sent out the invitations, and she took the security measures necessary to verify that we were who we said we were before she allowed us onto this very private site. It was meant as a place for us to meet each other, discuss our concerns about our soldiers, and just vent emotionally to someone who could understand us at this time in our lives.

The same principle was at work on this Web site that works so well for all those 12-step groups. We didn't have to say "walk a mile in my shoes." We were all walking the same mile together, so we knew without explanation what each other was feeling.

I already knew the site and had posted there before, but never about anything so raw as fear and stress and crying in public. But I went there and started a discussion. Some people responded. A couple of us bonded and started e-mailing with each other about our feelings. It was good to find someone who could say "Hey, I think our kids are in the same squad." It was in those private e-mails that we got to know each other so well.

We were a cross section of America with different political views, different spiritual views, and different social and economic levels. Yet, we bonded over this one connection as none of us was able to bond with our lifelong friends.

## If You Can't Find One, Form One

It may well be that no one has gone to the trouble to set up such a group for you. If not, you can do it yourself. Go to the rear detachment commander, explain what you have in mind, and ask for a list of next of kin. If he won't give you the list, ask him to contact them and ask them to contact you.

Or go through your contacts in the FRG. Most of the family members do not live near or on post and are not able to attend FRG meetings or take part in planned FRG activities. You do still need the emotional support though, perhaps even more than those wives on post who have their own social groups as a facet of their husband's military status.

You must be very careful to set up procedures to keep out any- one not associated with your group. You must be very careful to follow Op Sec (Operation Security) at all times. You must be very careful to follow any rules set up for you by the commander. If he demands the freedom to monitor your site, you should let him. Of course, you should never post a picture anywhere on the Internet of any military man or woman that shows his name or rank.

But you can create a secure Web site where members of your small community can check in with each other, exchange advice and information, shore each other up, and work on a few projects together that will take your minds off your worry and fear.

# What We Accomplished

It has happened throughout history. Put a bunch of worried women together, and you'll get a lot of food preparation, child care, and needlework done. Modern women have added to that list juggling a career, and our little group added packaging and mailing boxes to soldiers, praying together, and sharing our fear.

## Adopt a Soldier

The 66th had only been in place in Babylon and Karbala about a month when one of the soldiers lost all his underwear. Stories vary on how this happened. At first I was told it was all lost in the laundry. Later I heard something about an ambush and a bag of laundry lost in the fight.

In any case, we all heard about it, and we mobilized to get that boy clothed again. Word spread, and soon he had received several boxes that included, among other things, an awful lot of new underwear.

Some of us then began asking our own soldiers if they knew of anyone who didn't receive any mail at all. David told me about two or three people, and I sent boxes to them. Then I think several of us at the same time got the idea to try to ensure that every soldier in the 66th got regular mail from someone at home.

We began downright pestering our soldiers to give us names, and they came through. Some of us then contacted our own friends and family and set up our own Adopt a Soldier Program. It was highly successful, and soon packages were winging their way from strangers to our troops in Iraq.

You can do this too, either as a group or as an individual. Just start asking your soldier for names and needs. If you decide to be ambitious and match friends and family up with soldiers though, keep in mind the following rules:

- You should not share a soldier's address without that soldier's permission.

- You should not give a soldier's address to someone you don't know or don't have some connection with.

- Church groups are great for this sort of thing, as are sororities, schools, and any other philanthropic organization.

- When in doubt, send packages to the chaplain. He or she will be able to get them to the people who are most in need.

## Christmas Angel Project

We did so well with our "keep the soldiers supplied with mail" project that we were inspired to do something even more ambitious for the holiday season. If we could get people to adopt a soldier and send him or her occasional boxes, why couldn't we recruit enough people to adopt the entire company and make sure each soldier got at least one box of special holiday cheer during December.

It was quite an undertaking. We started out thinking that we could put together identical packages by mailing all the contents to a central location, where a few of us would get together to package them up. We soon figured out that the logistics and the cost of mailing all the contents to the central location and then to the soldiers in Iraq might be prohibitive, so we brainstormed another way to handle it.

Ideas and e-mails shot back and forth for a while. We had to have a current and complete list of all the soldiers in the company. We went to our friend Sgt. Sparks, explained our plans, and he came through for us. We had our list; now all we had to do was figure out how to make sure each one got a package.

After some discussion on the site, we decided on the following rules:

- Each of us in the core group would volunteer to be responsible for a certain number of soldiers.

  This didn't mean we would send a box to that soldier ourselves; only that we would recruit a volunteer from our circle of friends and family, or groups of people from our workplace or church who would accept responsibility for that soldier.

- We decided that each box should contain one major gift (for instance, a CD, a blanket, or a book); some candy and cookies and various treats, either homemade or purchased, any other small gifts or holiday items we chose to put in the box, and a Christmas ornament for the trees that were springing up all over Iraq. And a letter, of course.

I found a few family members and friends who were willing to sign up for the Christmas Angel program and ended up accepting responsibility for five soldiers, including my own. I was also sending packages to my cousins and a couple of other people who weren't in the 66th, so in total I was responsible for about 10 soldiers getting holiday packages.

My mother-in-law, sister-in-law, and some friends each accepted responsibility for putting together at least one box and mailing it so that it arrived in Iraq sometime in December.

Others were more ambitious. One mother of a soldier in the 66th accepted responsibility for 12 of the 66th soldiers. Her brother's church in Hendersonville, North Carolina, gathered the funds, worked to package the boxes, and got them ready to mail. They then gave her the boxes to address along with a check to cover the postage. The story of that church and that project was reported in the local newspaper.

Robin, the Web mistress, took up the slack. Her entire focus during the holiday season 2004 was on the soldiers in Iraq. Anyone who wasn't adopted by early November was simply taken under Robin's wing. She gathered her friends together and held day-long CARE package parties at her house, wrapping and packaging gifts.

You will find more about the Adopt a Soldier program and the Christmas Angel project in Chapter 3, "To the Post Office."

## Gifts for the Children

The soldiers often hand out treats to the local children. The 66th took responsibility for supplying a school in their area with school supplies. The kids enjoyed the attention, and some parents and family members also contributed to this effort.

This effort was just getting underway when our troops started returning home, but it is, in general, an ongoing project among many of the troops in Iraq. Check with your own soldier about whether it's appropriate for you to get involved in this effort as well.

## Individual Creativity

Some of us in the group put our own talents to work for the soldiers and each other. One mother made CDs for the entire group with slide shows of the 66th soldiers and background music. Very nice and awe-inspiring.

Of course, you've heard the stories of quilts and afghans and comforters being made and sent overseas. If you can sew or knit or crochet, there are all sorts of things you can make for the soldiers. Check out some of the support links listed in Chapter 3.

Or you could write a book about your experience.

# Sharing the Story of the War

One thing I did for friends and family was to send occasional updates on David's news and activities. I sent the e-mail to myself and bcc'd everybody I knew. It was an easy way to keep everyone who wanted to hear about David updated on his activities and to keep everyone I knew aware of the war and remind them to keep supporting the troops.

This practice of sending out general e-mails worked well for my family and friends. Of course, they often forwarded the messages on to their friends and acquaintances. My friend Susie told me that she forwarded the messages to her sister, who then forwarded them to all her co-workers. She said one man her sister worked with would occasionally ask, "Have you heard from David lately?" He said he didn't know us, but after receiving a few of these e-mails, he felt that he had a personal friend in Iraq.

If you decide to do something like this, just remember one thing: Do not put everyone's e-mail address in the To or CC box in the header of the e-mail. Use BCC. That way, not one of your addressees can see the e-mail address of the others, and if they forward your message, there will be no history with lots of people's contact information.

For the same reason, I never ever forwarded David's e-mail messages to anyone else. I copied and pasted pertinent parts of them into a new e-mail and sent that to close family and friends. But for general news of interest to several people, I wrote it myself and did not quote him directly. You must always keep in mind op sec and be very careful that you don't forward any information from the war zone or contact information for a soldier to anyone. This stuff can travel the world in seconds, and the enemy may well be monitoring messages you send. Be wary of sharing too much information. Keep it interesting but keep it general.

I know that seems a bit paranoid, but I figured I did not want to ever be guilty of providing aid and comfort to the enemy in any way. So I was careful about the information I shared with others. Following is an example of one of my general newsletters from Iraq:

To: Sandy

From: Sandy

Subject: News from Iraq

Date: Thursday, May 27, 2004 6:25 p.m.

David sent an e-mail yesterday. Nobody had heard from him in about 10 days, so we were starting to get worried. He said I should not worry because he's about as safe now as you can be in a war zone. When they go out on patrols now, there are always Apache helicopters nearby, and he said when they meet any kind of resistance, they just roll on through, then call in the Apaches to take out the attackers.

I told him I was kind of concerned about his mental health too because "how much death and destruction can you see without having it affect you." He said, "Mom, I'm too strong a person to let a little death and destruction bother me."

He said he thought maybe the bad guys recognize his company now and are afraid of them because every time they've attacked a patrol of MPs, they get hurt. So now he said the MPs can drive through an area and not get shot at and a few minutes later a convoy follows along, and they get ambushed. Either way, the Apaches take care of them. Plus, he said the area they patrol now is fairly clear and flat desert, so if anyone does come after them, they have plenty of warning.

He even said the food is getting better where he is. The biggest problem now is the heat. The temperature is around 105 every day. Since they are usually driving around during the hottest part of the day, he says when he gets back, he's so worn out from the heat, all he wants to do is eat, take a shower, and go to bed. The computers and telephones are a two-mile walk from where he stays, and it's just too hot to make the effort at the end of the day, so he doesn't try unless he gets a ride.

He also said that Camp Babylon, which is right next door to the ancient city of Babylon, is considered a "holy" site by the Shi'ites, so they don't ever fire mortars at the camp. (It seems to me that about every mile or so the Shi'ites have a "holy" site; I think it's just their way of saying "nyah, nyah, nyah, can't shoot us here 'cause this is a holy place." Personally, if I were in charge, I'd go after them that much harder.) Whatever the reason though, they aren't getting mortared at night, and that means they can sleep, and that's a good thing. Aren't they lucky to have perched themselves in one of those holy spots? Maybe they should declare the whole damn country to be holy. Then where would all the guys with the bombs go? Oh, wait, they were hiding guns and ammo in the mosques in Karbala. So we have to respect their holy sites, but they don't have to. They are using our political correctness to their advantage, aren't they? And we're falling for it.

So today he called, and here's what he said when I talked to him:

He went to the computers and there was a line of about 20 people waiting to use them. So he went into headquarters and said that he had to call home because he hadn't been able to call in three weeks. The Army likes for them to call home because they don't like to get phone calls from angry mothers saying their kid hasn't called home in two weeks. So the Sgt in HQ let him use the satellite phone to call me. For once, it was a good connection, so we had a nice little chat.

He pretty much said the same things he'd said in his e-mail except for the following little bit of excitement:

Today they were driving toward Baghdad on one of the main supply routes. They passed a truck sitting on the opposite side of the road. One guy was digging a hole by the road. Another one had something in his hands, which he dropped when he saw them drive by. David thought they looked kind of guilty, so he radioed to the squad leader and said "Did you see those guys acting suspiciously back there?" They sent someone back to investigate, and found a 150-mm bomb that they were getting ready to set up as an IED; that's what the one guy had dropped. They arrested the two guys, of course, and defused the bomb. I'm sure somewhere there's an Iraqi family wringing their hands on Al-Jazeera today, saying, "The Americans just kidnapped them; they were going into town to look for work, and they disappeared." Right.

He has taken some pictures to mail home, and he says they're all packaged up ready to send. He just hasn't had them with him when he's had a chance to go to the PX where the post office is. When I get them, I'll send them with an e-mail, but it will probably be at least a month before that happens.

I especially asked him for pictures of the soldiers you all adopted.

I did not send these e-mails with any regularity, but I did it several times during the year David was in Iraq. I like to think it helped enlighten everyone I know about the daily down and dirty activities in a war zone. And I hope it helped to keep many people consciously aware that we have soldiers who are doing a dirty job in a dangerous and uncomfortable place.

# What We Got Back

The point I want to make by writing this book is that you can survive the deployment of your loved one, you can survive the fear and anxiety if you:

1.  Try to put those scary numbers in perspective and not dwell on the danger.

2.  Arm yourself with information.

3.  Stay busy with a project of your own in support of the troops.

4.  Find others who share your concerns and stay in touch with them.

I put the numbers and news stories and statistics in perspective by finding out as much as I could about the geography and areas of unrest in Iraq and where my soldier son fit into that picture. The more informed I was about the whole situation, the more control I had over my sense of fear and foreboding.

My project was CARE packages and mail, and I devoted a great deal of time and expense gathering food, hygiene, and fun items to send packages to the soldiers I knew (at least one a week, often more than that).

Finally, and most important of all, I found a group of people who could support me at 3:00 a.m. when I could not sleep and was just searching for a word of comfort. We'll always be battle buddies, just as our soldiers are lifelong battle buddies. When you "walk through the valley of the shadow of death" together, you learn what it really means to say, "I trust you with my life."

I'll finish this book with the words of a few of those lifelong battle buddies I met last year:

# Karen

I guess what I got from the group was several things. I am sure I will think of more later. The first was how hearing all the other stuff we had to endure while we were in such a state of fear was actually comforting. I know a few of us had family members die, we had awful snows, some of us dealt with marital strife, just making ends meet, illnesses we all had due to our stress, close calls with older relatives, and the daily stresses we all live with.

What did I get from our group? Survival, simple, wonderful, blessed survival. I got support from those who knew what I felt without words. I got lifetime friends and words of wisdom from some wise and kind women.

What did I learn? That I had friends I knew I could come home in the evening and get on the computer with, and with that I could make it through days of unendurable stress. That I did not have to fear I was missing the news or knowledge of what was going on because Robin called me at work to keep me abreast if anything happened that I needed to know about. And I learned that you can get up and go to work, you can carry on with your regular routine, when your mind and half your heart is in Iraq.

Later I learned how very scared I really had been when a full three months after he got home, I finally let go and let myself realize he was home and ALIVE.

# Robin (The Web Mistress)

I learned a lot more than I could ever have imagined, mostly a new understanding of the common ground people share during difficult times, regardless of our individuality; this understanding bred patience when normally I wouldn't have had any, or maybe tolerance is a better word.

I can put aside political, spiritual, all those belief differences, when reality is sitting on my head. Sometimes folks on the site would speak from an ill-informed stance, or a prejudice, and unless it was an outright form of abuse to someone, I finally figured out that this was their belief, and though I may not like it, it was pointless to argue. I just let it go; it didn't have to live in my world, it was simply another person's viewpoint. At times, this was a double-edged sword, but I learned I did not need to be a martyr. I just needed to be gently firm, and to make it clear what was and was not okay, even in the most fearful of situations.

I found I had much more courage than I realized, and part of that courage was understanding that I was afraid, but I had to keep moving forward, keeping foremost in my mind the goal: to see our soldiers again, safe and sound, to see my son, safe and sound.

Fear is one hell of a motivator, in both a positive and a negative sense. Everyone deals differently, and for the most part, there simply is no correct way, just a personal way to handle fear, much like grief. I would not have fared well at all without the support and the work (keeping me busy) of the site.

I looked forward to any word about any soldier, because once I had a connection, my narrow viewpoint of my son being in a war zone changed to everyone's child being in harm's way; it increased my worry, but amazingly, it increased my ability to handle that worry. I don't think it was a misery loves company thing; I think it was more of a like-mindedness, and with that similar situation we were all in came a need that led to caring beyond my own.

I also learned that people can and will continue to be who they are regardless of what is going on in life, the good, the bad, and the ugly.

I also learned that once the danger and fear are removed, people will go back to life as they know it, some routine, some new ways of living, and some more mistakes; but usually with a better take on how to handle some things.

I found I cannot let go of how I feel about war in general, and I am focused on what will happen to our soldiers. I think this is a continuum, and will be a theme for the rest of my life. I know that was the hardest year of my life, trying to make it through each day, constant (no kidding) worrying, worrying, and worrying. It was harder than the death of my husband. I learned that unless a person is directly affected by a situation, such as war, birth, death, etc. there is no empathy, rather a polite concern, that doesn't make its mark.

I found a grace I have never seen before, and ebb and flow of support that was natural, I believe, between parents of children in danger, and a respect for my fellow travelers through very difficult times.

## Lori

Yesterday when I saw the tornado damage in Indiana, I thought of you, my sister. Then I thought, "No, this is too far south, I think." But I guess that is it. That is my commentary on our group. I do think a very strong bond grew between us all. Praying for your children, hearing of their journeys, praying for you all and your worried hearts and minds. I grew from your strengths and your love for your children. You became my family--closer than family because my deep worry often isolated me from even my nearest relatives. The members of our Web site all had one single overriding concern—to see those soldiers come home safe and sound. Nowhere else did I find such like-minded people, and you all became my family.

You and Robin and Karen were loving and caring to me on a personal level that went beyond the situation we were dealing with in terms of our children being in Iraq. It is hard to say that because when they were there, that is all that mattered to me.

As you know though, I did have other struggles, and I think without the three of you and Jessica and others on the site encouraging me and just "sitting" with me through our year-long prayer vigil, I would have snapped like a twig.

In fact, I miss the sweet communion that we shared during that time though I do not miss the reason. (Is this one of the most repeated phrases written by any of us since they came home?) I think the intensity of the personal storm of your child being in a war zone calls for a close knit group to support you and I am so thankful I had that with you all.

# Where Two Are Gathered Together

Probably no one readily remembers now the significance of January 30, 2005. Much has happened in Iraq and elsewhere since that day. I remember it as the night I stayed awake all night with 10 or 12 members of our Web site. We stayed awake to pray for peace during the first Iraqi election. I also remember the next day when all of our soldiers were unharmed, and very little violence had happened during a day in Iraq when much violence had been predicted. A low voter turnout had also been predicted, but the Iraqis came out to vote in record numbers.

It brought tears to my eyes to see them standing in line, literally risking their lives for democracy, while here in this country we are lucky to get half the eligible adult population to even register to vote and so many of us can find better things to do on election day. I swore I would never miss another election.

Our soldiers had spent the weeks leading up to that election helping to deliver ballots to polling places, and we were especially worried for their safety. The 66th was due to start home within two weeks of that election, and it just seemed extra scary to us to know that they had to endure this extra bit of danger after 11 months of patrolling the already dangerous and hostile streets of Babylon, Karbala, Hilla, and Najaf, with occasional trips into Baghdad along a road deemed the "most dangerous highway in the world."

So we decided that we would hold a prayer vigil. We'd light candles, pray alone in our homes, and join together in a chat room. Of course, we weren't the only ones to hold a prayer vigil that night. Many military families and many churches did just what we were doing—stayed up all night to pray.

It must have worked too because that was one of the most peaceful elections ever held in a developing country like Iraq. I believe that our prayers made a difference that night, and I became convinced of the power of prayer. I don't want to ever forget what I learned that night.

# Wrapping It Up

On February 22,2005, the 66th MP Company returned to Ft. Lewis after a year in Babil Province in Iraq. All but one: Spc. Jesse Buryj was lost on May 5, 2004. Their homecoming was bittersweet because of the loss. We all learned so much during that year, soldiers and families alike, about what we are able to endure, but one of our number had to learn to live with the unendurable.

This book is dedicated to Jesse's mom, Peggy. May she find comfort in faith. May she find comfort in knowing that her son will live on in the memories of all who were a part of the 66th MP Company in 2004.

# Care Package Suggestions Checklist

## Food

### Breakfast

- ❏ Cereal
- ❏ Instant oatmeal
- ❏ Breakfast bars
- ❏ Protein and energy bars
- ❏ PopTarts

### Lunch and Dinners

- ❏ Tuna (best in an envelope)
- ❏ Chicken salad or turkey salad (in envelopes)
- ❏ Chicken salad or tuna salad (in kits with relishes, mayo)
- ❏ Beef jerky (make sure does not contain pork)

- ❏ Peanut butter
- ❏ Jelly or jam
- ❏ Crackers and breadsticks
- ❏ Cheese crackers
- ❏ Spreadable cheese
- ❏ Canned stew and other canned goods
- ❏ Freeze-dried meals
- ❏ Ramen noodles

## Condiments

- ❏ Mayonnaise (individual packets)
- ❏ Salad dressing (individual packets)
- ❏ Salsa
- ❏ Pickle Relish (individual packets)

## Snacks

- ❏ Cookies (store bought)
- ❏ Cookies (home made)
- ❏ Rice Krispie squares
- ❏ Trail mix
- ❏ Candy, gum, mints, licorice, Life Savers (avoid chocolate during hot months)
- ❏ Cup cakes (packaged with preservatives) (Hostess Twinkies, Ding Dongs, Dolly Madison Zingers, Little Debbie)
- ❏ Individually wrapped fruit snacks
- ❏ Sunflower seeds, nuts

❏ Bread sticks

❏ Pringle's-type canned potato chips

❏ Chip dip (one that doesn't need refrigeration)

❏ Microwave popcorn

## Beverages

❏ Kool-Aid

❏ Gatorade powder mix

❏ Instant coffee and tea

## Utensils

❏ Bowl

❏ Fork, Knife, and Spoon

❏ Paper towels

❏ Zip-lock sandwich bag

# Toiletries

## General Hygiene Needs:
- ❑ Shampoo (unscented)
- ❑ Conditioner (unscented)
- ❑ Soap
- ❑ Body powder (spill-proof container)
- ❑ Deodorant (unscented)
- ❑ Moisturizer or body lotion; hand lotion or cream (unscented)
- ❑ Waterless hand cleaner
- ❑ Toothpaste
- ❑ Toothbrush
- ❑ Floss
- ❑ Mouthwash
- ❑ Mouthwash strips

## Especially needed in the desert
- ❑ Saline nasal spray
- ❑ Visine
- ❑ Lip balm or Chap Stick
- ❑ Hard candy or throat lozenges

## First Aid Items
- ❑ Aspirin, ibuprofen, or Tylenol in individual packs
- ❑ Vitamins
- ❑ Band-Aids

❑ Neosporin

❑ Insect repellent (unscented)

❑ Sun block (unscented)

❑ Rubbing alcohol

## Foot care items (very important):

❑ Moleskin

❑ Foot powder ( Gold Bond in the blue can is best)

❑ Insoles

❑ Foot soak

❑ Nail clippers

❑ Loofah

❑ Pumice stone

❑ Emery boards

## Shaving stuff for men and women

❑ Razor

❑ Razor blades

❑ Shaving cream or gel

❑ Electric shaver

## Feminine hygiene needs:

❑ Tampons and Pads

❑ Feminine hygiene spray

❑ Panty liners

❑ Midol

❑ Individually packed facial gels

# Useful Housekeeping Items

- ❏ Extra flashlight
- ❏ Good toilet paper
- ❏ Baby Wipes or Wet Ones in individual packets
- ❏ Phone Cards
- ❏ Kleenex
- ❏ Q-tips
- ❏ Wash cloths
- ❏ Towels
- ❏ Hygiene bags
- ❏ Fly swatters
- ❏ Back scratchers and bath brushes
- ❏ Duct tape
- ❏ Super glue
- ❏ Sewing kits
- ❏ Safety pins
- ❏ Scissors
- ❏ Velcro
- ❏ Clorox wipes
- ❏ Mini mag lites
- ❏ Batteries
- ❏ Stick-up tap lights
- ❏ Office supplies (pens, paper, and envelopes)
- ❏ Clear Packing Tape

# Entertainment Items

- ❑ Books
- ❑ Magazines
- ❑ Hometown newspaper subscriptions
- ❑ Crossword and word search puzzle books
- ❑ Crayons, markers, coloring books, construction paper
- ❑ Store bought or homemade holiday items
- ❑ Frisbees
- ❑ Nerf footballs and basketballs
- ❑ Card games
- ❑ Dice and dominoes
- ❑ Board games (travel type)
- ❑ CDs, DVDs
- ❑ A laptop
- ❑ CDs or tapes with messages from family members, CDs of favorite local radio programs
- ❑ Letters and Pictures and Cards
- ❑ Drawings and Letters from Children
- ❑ Gameboys

## Especially for the Hot, Dry Climate

- ❑ Ice tea (gallon jug, teabags, sugar)
- ❑ Squirt guns, kiddie pools, and water balloons
- ❑ Ice packs
- ❑ Freezer pops

## Miscellaneous Handy Items

- ❏ Wrap around sunglasses
- ❏ Detergent
- ❏ Disposable cameras
- ❏ Egg crate mattress pad
- ❏ Pillow and sheets

# Clothing

- ❏ T-shirts
- ❏ Sweat wicking socks and underwear
- ❏ Black Socks

# Tobacco Products

- ❏ Cigarettes
- ❏ Chew
- ❏ Other

# Forbidden Items (do not send)

- ❏ Alcohol
- ❏ Pork products
- ❏ Pornography
- ❏ Bulk religious pamphlets

# Mom's Field Guide:
## What You Need to Know to Make It Through Your Loved One's Military Deployment

## <u>Order a copy for a friend</u>

Go to

http://www.momsfieldguide.com

or to pay by check, order form below.

Please send me _____ copy(ies) of
*Mom's Field Guide: What You Need to Know to Make It Through Your Loved One's Military Deployment* published by Warrior Angel Press/Publishing Alternatives

mail check to:  **Marian Hartsough Associates**
1285 Stratford Avenue, Suite G262
Dixon, California 95620
866-221-8408

Name _____

Address _____

State _____ Zip _____ Phone _____

Join us online at:

## While Our Children Serve
http://www.whileourchildrenserve.com

Do you have a family member who is being deployed? Find the resources and information you need to make it through.

Do you want to help support the soldiers? We have places to go where your efforts will really make a difference, great organizations that will help you:

- Send a care package
- Send a card to a serviceperson
- Donate frequent flyer miles
- Contribute to scholarship funds for children of fallen soldiers
- And more

Sandy Doell
author of *Mom's Field Guide*

Marian Hartsough
publisher
Warrior Angel Press/
Publishing Alternatives

Printed in the United States
209136BV00001B/82/A